Trade Secrets

Trade Secrets

Classic and Contemporary Surfaces and Finishes

Jocasta Innes

Principal photography by
Mark Gatehouse and David George

Weidenfeld & Nicolson

Text © Jocasta Innes 1995
Photographs © George Weidenfeld & Nicolson, 1995, except as otherwise stated

Jocasta Innes has asserted her right
to be identified as the Author of this work

First published in 1995 by George Weidenfeld & Nicolson Ltd
The Orion Publishing Group, Orion House,
5 Upper St. Martin's Lane, London WC2H 9EA

British Library Catalogue-in-Publication Data
A catalogue record for this book is available from the British Library

ISBN 0 297 833405

Edited by Judy Spours
Designed by Steven Wooster
Photographs by Mark Gatehouse and David George
Project co-ordination by Sarah Curran

Printed and bound in Italy

Frontispiece: Fibrous plaster casts in the workshop of Butchers
Plastering Specialists Ltd., London.

Contents

Introduction

IN DESCRIBING THIS BOOK, I find myself explaining that it is really about 'materials', a handily loose definition that can include ingredients as various as mud, needle-gunned concrete and 22 carat gold leaf so gossamer fine that a sneeze will send it flying. Why materials? My justification for this enthusiasm, which borders on obsession, is that I need to track what I see and admire (or even hate) back to its earliest origins. I want to know much more about what this built environment of ours is made of, why it evolved as it did and what we may have thrown out in the late twentieth century, through ignorance or negligence, in the natural and understandable desire to keep up or ahead of what science and technology and commercial competition are delivering. In researching this book, some of my instinctive prejudices have been

Right: A limewashed bedroom in an old Devon cob-built cottage. The creamy yellow colour and gentle matt surface of tinted limewash look entirely appropriate as a background to stripped pine, old rugs and interesting pictures. The huge old fireplace was discovered, with some of its late medieval decoration still intact, when the cottage was restored recently. Cheaper than tiles, the strong geometric design in black and white is an idea worth copying. Lime render first, then paint over in black and white limewash. A plain white limewash band does duty for a fireplace surround.

Left: Criss-cross perforations make diamond patterns across lime plastering in an old French farmhouse. This is the sort of thing one could do with a pastry wheel or a ravioli cutter while the plaster is still soft enough to take impressions. The lines are a bit skewed but the effect is good, a bit like pargeting without the Tudor Roses.

confounded. I now have no doubt at all that twentieth-century concrete, still labouring under a cloud of misunderstanding, is extraordinarily flexible, with the potential of joining the list of noble materials – marble, stone, bronze, hardwoods – as a grand, handsome, low-maintenance building material ideally suited to the requirements of modern architecture in its most daring conceptual flights.

In parallel with this discovery came others of a quite different order. Simple old mud, I now realise, is still a viable, cheap and ideally plastic building material, in use since pre-history, yet still standing today, the world over. Think of adobe, of English 'cob' cottages, of French *pisé de terre*. In desert climates mud building needs little protection. In wet northern climates, it requires intelligent support in the way of projecting eaves (usu-ally thatch), porous renders and points inside and out. Historically these are always lime-based, because building limes are naturally capable of absorb-ing and then releasing moisture: the lime system 'breathes'. Building limes have proved to be the key not only to understanding and respecting the old building practices, but to recreating some far more sophisticated finishes, such as marmorino, one of many ancient Italian stucco surfaces, used since at least Pompeian times, which have entered the folklore of decorative painters today. Once the lime technology, not so much mysterious as tricky in operation, is fully understood, a whole range of ancient traditional skills and practices opens up. In this book we have tried to de-mystify lime technology as far as possible, showing, for example, how to apply a polished lime stucco; how to make and colour a limewash from putty lime; and how lime renders were used for purposes as various as decorative shellwork or a straightforward porous render on an old cottage exterior.

Traditional gesso is becoming trendy as a wall paint. Applied warm, it dries with a fine, silky texture, ideal for absorbing drifts of subtle watercolour to give the extraordinary, mysterious effect shown here in the London home of an artist/dealer.

This selection of picture frames by London contemporary artist Howard Raybould signals a new direction in decorated furniture: lots of colour but apparently no paint, at least not paint so you would know it was there. Raybould uses a variety of media and methods to achieve these pure, vivid effects – tube paints rubbed on and off, stains, waxes, heat, polishing. The feel is wood, the grain is wood but the colour is something else.

This is not simply a nostalgic initiative. It is significant that the most modern of architects are re-evaluating the usefulness of this ancient building material. One advantage of standing where we are, on the threshold of a new millennium, is surely that we can take a longer, more dispassionate, historical perspective, re-evaluating the merits and disadvantages of materials used everywhere since earliest recorded time, and deciding whether or not they still have a serious role to play in an alarmingly fast-moving contemporary world.

Raw Surfaces

Catching hold of the coat-tail of an idea always makes me want to know more about the coat: what it is made of, why it is made *that way*. Thus an obsession with pure colour led me to *buon fresco*, which led me to lime, which led to a whole lot of topics explored in this book. But along with the ancient building material of lime, it seemed necessary to explore others for comparison, whether as simple as mud, or as sophisticated as high-specification concrete: pre-cast, needle-gunned, sand-blasted, white as limestone or colourful as nougat. The world out there is changing; this is a truism, but perhaps less recognized is the undoubted fact that it is not inexorably rushing forward, as our nineteenth-century Utopian forebears firmly believed. We stand back for a longer, dispassionate and questioning view of where we are, in the light – or shadow – of history and tradition, and of current ecological and social concerns. Building limes have become fashionable, not simply because they offer a key to so many otherwise hermetic skills, or because they are 'green' and somehow organic, but because they also open up viable alternatives in intermediate technology. It is to be hoped that these are building materials the Third World can master and afford – not to rush up swaggering tower blocks, or human hencoops, but so that ordinary people can be decently housed, wherever and however they live.

I T ALL STARTS WITH THE RAW MATERIALS, their cost, potential, soundness in use and over time. People are increasingly concerned about what is called 'the built environment', wanting to preserve, enhance and balance it. In this section we look at some of the surprisingly natural materials, acted upon over thousands of years by human intelligence, creativity and courage, of which it is constructed, and which are still in use today. Old materials are put to new uses, and new materials used to extend old concepts in a very dynamic building environment.

Mud as a building material

PERHAPS THE MOST STRIKING feature of mud buildings is their joyfully sculptural quality, vividly exemplified in the range, mostly Third World in origin, shown here. These are primarily dwellings, undoubtedly made from the cheapest building material available in a tradition so ancient that its origins are unguessable. Something of the potter's delight in making, moulding and decorating his earth-begotten material shines out from the humble vernacular structures and is strangely liberating to wealthier cultures obliged to take their building initiatives so solemnly and seriously. Even where mud building is cheaply accessible, individual pride and imagination still make their mark. It must always have been important to distinguish your mud house from its neighbours, pressing in pebbles like the early Mesopotamians, or painting or impressing the surface with intricate and bold patterns, as they do in Africa to this day.

Nomadic tribes threw up temporary shelters and moved on. With the first mud structures came the idea of settlement and community. Mud was the only free material to build with in parts of the world too arid for timber, too poor to quarry stone and too primitive to embrace the technology of fired earth bricks. In the right climate, even an inclement one, mud was far more practical than can be readily grasped by those who live in the age of concrete, steel and glass. It was also capable of aesthetic development. Mud houses grow out of their soil, their shapes rounded and natural, their textures profoundly satisfying to a modern eye. But it would be wrong to suppose that mud building was always crudely *ad hoc*. It was early recognized that it was more satisfactory when the walls were raised on stone foundations and were themselves hugely thick and durable, providing insulation against fierce climates.

Mud, or earth, building methods can be roughly classified into three types. The simplest, applicable to British cob or wattle and daub as well as North African mud-houses, consists of pitching moist clay in layers onto a marked-out foundation and ramming the rough and pliable material down to compact it solidly, layer by layer, until the walls were raised to a livable ceiling height. With the help of timber joists, the building might rise higher, to a second storey. If the mud contained binding agents such as straw, grass or dung, it proved more cohesive and durable. The sheer weight of the basic material kept these structures standing. They tended to have thick walls, three feet in Northern

Europe, where extra weatherproofing was also added – projecting eaves of thatch to throw off rain, a coat of lime render inside and out.

In France, particularly, a more rationalized use of mud is evident historically. *Pisé de terre* was used widely in south-western France: barely moist mud was rammed down between timber 'forms', giving a sharper look and possibly more durable structure to French vernacular mud housing. Recently, a courageous but quite unskilled couple embarked on the restoration of a French farmhouse, scooping the soil from a convenient patch (sandy as well as clayey and not too wet proved ideal), the mud pit gradually becoming, as must often have happened in rural areas, a naturally filling puddled clay pond.

The third method, open to those living in a dry, hot climate, was to fashion mud bricks of varying shapes, left to dry and harden in the sun and cemented together with a mud mortar. The technique has been used the world over, but Mexican adobe is the best-known example. To most Westerners visiting a refurbished adobe building of pretensions – with

Mud construction gives a North African tenement the look of something organic, a termite hill perhaps, together with a free-form picturesqueness of outline. Closer examination, however, shows that these wonderfully lively dwellings conform to certain disciplines, as in fenestration and the siting of chimneys. Buildings like these are most probably constructed from dried mud bricks, adobe-style, using wet mud both as mortar and final exterior render.

ceramic tiled floor, deep window embrasures, smoothly rounded whitewashed surfaces – it must come as a shock to discover how primitive the structure is in its ancient, mud-brick construction. Perhaps the most visually distinctive feature of mud architecture in general, and the one which has influenced a number of contemporary designers, is the satisfying roundedness of its surfaces, inside and out. Handy alcoves can be hollowed out from massively thick walls, and friendly, rustic kitchen areas seem to follow on naturally from such an adaptive technology. The sculptural effect of rough plastered units is very appealing today, in contrast to the high-specification tightness of so many contemporary interiors.

Flints

FLINTS ARE NODULES OF EXCEPTIONALLY hard stone, the purest form of native silica, found mainly in chalky soil. They look uncommonly like bones, being covered with a dense, white, chalky layer and often knobbly in shape. Knapped, or split, the flint emerges as a lustrous, dark surface, more like opaque glass than stone. Flints have been used for walling since Roman times, either on their own or in courses set between brick or stone. The usual construction method was to raise two flint courses some distance apart, using lime mortar to bed them securely and lime mortar packed out with rubble to fill the space between. The use of flints for walling is a nice instance of recycling, converting the heaps of flints which farmers dug out of their land into solid, enduring structures.

Mud architecture, like plasticine while wet, has always lent itself to surface decoration – painted, carved, impressed with moulds, or patchworked with shards of pottery, patterns of pebbles, seashells. The strikingly decorated building shown here is in Ghana and shows how the simplest building type often exhibits the most ambitious and complex exterior treatment.

Used raw, flints create an interesting surface, especially when offset by smooth bricks, but their real beauty as a building material emerges when they are knapped. In Britain, Suffolk and Norfolk are the traditional centres of flint knapping, and splendid examples can be seen in these two counties' parish churches, such as those at Clare, Lavenham and Crome, many of them dating from early in the Perpendicular period (*c.* 1300-1540).

Knapping a flint presents a dark, glossy, faceted surface, usually round in shape, which catches the light to give their peculiar darkly glinting appearance. Packed tightly and mortared, they present a rich, dark, irregular surface not unlike pebble mosaic. Knapping, like slate cutting, is an old skill which requires knack as much as muscle, and flints must have needed several blows to present a flattish 'fair face'.

A few specialist lime centres run courses teaching the proper way to knap flints and lay them, as found, in construction work. The chief demand for flint work is in building garden walls or in the repair of old flint and brick buildings, but there are signs that the current generation of architects are revaluing this interesting and handsome building material.

Pargeting

THE WORD DERIVES FROM OLD FRENCH *parjeter*, to throw over or into, but traditionally pargeting describes a style of exterior decorative plasterwork which became fashionable on timber-framed buildings in England, and specifically East Anglia, during the mid-sixteenth century. The infill between the exposed timbers of these vernacular buildings, often sizable village houses, consisted of a variety of materials – mud, wattle and daub, lath and plaster – all of which needed protective lime rendering. By then relief decorative plasterwork had been introduced as an element in the interiors of great Elizabethan houses, and one can hazard a link between these and the bold, crude, but wonderfully lively sculpturing in wet lime

Cob is a traditional form of mud building used in south-western England for centuries. When Devon builder Kevin McCabe needed to extend his existing cob cottage, cob was the appropriate material to choose, and he had the technical skills and knowledge to do it. The earth was dug nearby. Kevin and one assistant pitched the walls up a layer at a time, treading and ramming them to compact them firmly. The walls are over two feet thick and have the gently rounded line which is such an attractive feature of mud building in every culture.

plaster that distinguishes so many buildings in East Anglia at this period. The decorative vocabulary is simplified, usually vigorous plant forms, but there is a striking similarity in style and execution, a mix of local and familiar motifs, such as stags and roses, with Italianate ornament, such as vines and grapes.

Skilled local plasterers would have worked in lime and sand mixes to produce parget ornament in low relief. To support ornament projecting several inches from the base, they would have banged in nails, maybe connected by wire, to form a rough armature. As the metal parts rusted, the oxidization spread through the plasterwork, acting as a stiffening agent. Over a base of 'coarse stuff' – lime worked with sharp sand or grit – they would have applied a finishing coat of finely textured lime render to allow finer, detailed modelling. Once dry and hard, the whole surface, with its bold decoration, would have been limewashed in white or a local colour so that the parget decoration leapt out when the sunlight struck it from a low angle, as on spring and autumn days.

A humbler form of pargeting, where still soft and impressionable render is impressed with carved moulds, was also used. Moulds, often of boxwood because of its dense, fine grain and hardness, were carved out in reverse. Pressed or hammered into a still yielding render, they left the impress of a low-relief design. Tudor roses and geometric patterns were popular, lending sixteenth- and seventeenth-century small houses and cottages a distinctive charm. The ancient craft survives, and perhaps it will not be long before master pargeters offer hand-modelled decoration in traditional materials as well as the run of impressed Tudor roses and the like which are already being employed.

Building Lime

HISTORICALLY, THE MOST IMPORTANT CEMENT was unquestionably lime, used the world over for thousands of years. That so much of the ancient world survives is due to favourable climatic conditions and skilled construction, but also, in large measure, to the properties of 'building limes', so called to distinguish them from many other uses of lime, such as in tanning, glass blowing or agriculture. After more than a century of eclipse, building limes are coming back into favour, not only with conservationists but also with architects, high-tech architects at that. Sir Michael Hopkins' new Glyndebourne Opera House in Sussex uses lime mortar throughout.

Lime is a versatile and (to a non-chemist) mysterious substance. It is made by burning quarried limestone in special kilns at high temperatures. What remains after

Knapped flint cut geometrically presents a smooth, subtly light-reflecting surface on a wall of the parish church at Long Melford, Suffolk.

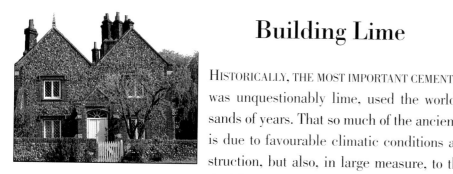

Above: The demure tweedy or 'knitted' texture of flint walling combined with red bricks is one of the more charming legacies of Victorian house building in rural Britain.

Left: Shellwork and delicate 'scales' of knapped flint are combined here on the façade of an eighteenth-century shell house in Hatfield Forest, Essex.

firing is a soft, powdery substance like coagulated detergent powder, known as 'lump lime'. It looks innocent but it is dangerous – this is quicklime. When lump lime is 'slaked' by adding water to it, a fierce chemical reaction occurs, converting it to 'putty lime'. The drama of the slaking is one of the things that makes lime fascinating (see page 35).

Under a layer of water, lime putty keeps, indeed improves, growing more workable, for decades. Lime hardens by carbonation, a chemical reaction in which the slaked lime combines with carbon dioxide in the air to revert to its primary state, calcium carbonate, in effect limestone. This process continues long after drying as we recognize it is complete. Nevertheless, lime cement remains 'soft' compared to modern cement finishes. Its great advantage as a mortar is that this inherent 'softness' allows the building fabric to move and settle without cracking, as is strikingly illustrated at Glyndebourne, where the use of lime mortar throughout obviates the need for the expansion joints customary in large modern buildings, where contraction and expansion of the fabric as a result of heating and cooling leads to tiny but significant movement in the structure.

Lime's porosity, its famous breathing property, is best seen on a lime render on a rainy day. Lime render wetted darkens at once as moisture is sucked into the surface, paling again as it dries. In a lime-rendered cob cottage with limewashed interior, a heavy rainfall even brings damp, darker patches up on the inside walls as the moisture passes through the fabric and out into the atmosphere. This sight gladdens a conservationist heart, because it demonstrates that the breathing system is in place and functioning.

Left: A detail of the façade of the fifteenth-century Priest's House in Clare, Suffolk.

Below: The house seen whole, showing how richly this type of surface decoration was used to distinguish an unpretentious, timber-framed rural house of the period. Pargeted walls like this would always have been limewashed, as protection as well as for visual appeal.

Concrete

AS IS CONFUSINGLY THE WAY with many basic building terms, the words mortar and concrete are often used almost interchangeably because their uses and functions so often overlap historically. Broadly speaking, mortar is the binding cementitious agent used to bond rubble, crushed brick, sand and a variety of other aggregates, to form concrete, which is really a man-made stone – hard, durable, relatively impervious to climatic conditions. Anything stone could do could be done more cheaply, rapidly and in some cases more efficiently with concrete. Because of its plasticity before hardening, concrete can be cast, on or off site, in 'forms' (like gigantic moulds, usually of timber) to fulfil exacting specifications. Today an immense pre-cast, reinforced concrete building element can be accurate to within 2 mm, so that it slots into its allotted space as tightly as the marble columns that support the Parthenon in Athens.

Concrete – pre-cast, reinforced – is so much the servant of twentieth-century architecture, at both its best, for example, Sydney Opera House, and at its worst as in the grim urban

Carved wooden moulds or stamps (like giant butter stamps) pressed into still soft lime render give the tidy, geometric surfaces shown on a row of East Anglian village houses painted in soft earthy tones. This form of pargeting, less demanding than the hand-moulded type, is still much used in the area, though sadly more often on hard, modern cement.

landscape of low cost tenements ringing major cities everywhere from Paris to Peking, that it is hard to take in that concrete is an ancient discovery on the one hand, and a potentially noble material in the right circumstances on the other.

Until as recently as the nineteenth century, concrete was made only with lime mortar, lime acting as the cementitious material. The Romans advanced early concrete practice significantly, using rubble 'hearting' or filling bound with lime mortar, as a cheaper sandwich filling between two surfaces of dressed stone. They worked out ingenious ways of using concrete in vault construction, as at the Pantheon in Rome. But, perhaps most impressively, given that their understanding of *opus caementicium* can only have been empirical, they developed the use of 'hydraulic' lime cement (which enables concrete to set under water) and a range of 'pozzolans' or special aggregates, such as volcanic ash from Pozzuoli (hence the name) which gave extra hardness and faster setting times to an inherently problematic, unpredictable type of mortar, at least in a context of huge, costly public works such as viaducts, breakwaters, bridges or foundations for major buildings.

Innovative, pragmatic and enduring as Roman lime concrete has proved itself to be, there was inevitably an ongoing demand for an equivalent or substitute that could be manufactured commercially, under controlled conditions, to yield a predictable and reliable result. The demand peaked, unsurprisingly, during the Industrial Revolution in Britain. Portland Cement, now known as OPC (Ordinary Portland Cement) is the invention of an Englishman, Joseph Aspdin, patented in 1824, named after its supposed resemblance when set to Portland stone. Aspdin discovered, by analysis and intuition, that it was the naturally occurring impurities – clay, magnesium, silica and the like, in quarried limestone that accounted

Below: A long shot of architect John Outram's 'Doodlecrete', used on his astonishingly colourful new building in Cambridge University to house The Judge Institute of Management Studies. Doodlecrete, his own descriptive name, is a sort of latter-day version of encaustic tile technique, using white concrete 'piped' into the blue stained concrete base, then scraped and etched clean for a strong inlaid contrast effect.

for the special properties of slaked lime, such as hydraulicity and strength. Aspdin formulated a process, based on a formula now universally applicable, whereby the necessary natural ingredients, combined in the right proportions and fired and refined under mass-market conditions, yielded a cement that behaved to order. It hardened and bonded within a given time and even in watery conditions, as in the massive pad fountain it supplied for the Houses of Parliament in London.

This invention, startling in its implications for our own age, was not immediately recognized fully. No twentieth-century architect has proposed a proper memorial to Aspdin, their pioneer enabler. The French, shrewdly, seized first on this technological breakthrough. But the Aspdin invention awaited a further discovery, also British – the patent of a Midlands workman in the mid-century of rods of mild steel, inserted into a concrete element before hardening on or off site, providing an additional, tensile strength. Once more it was French engineers who seized on the possibilities of a discovery whose twentieth-century applications are limitless. It is paradoxical that two relatively unknown Englishmen of humble background indirectly fathered a school of architecture which includes the acknowledged masterpieces of construction of our times.

Debased by so much opportunistic commercial development, concrete has become a layman's term of abuse in the late twentieth century. But architects, including the very best, love it, respect it, depend upon it as their springboard to invention. It is tough, requires low maintenance, is climatically stable and potentially handsome. The aesthetic development of concrete as building material over the past twenty years is little recognized. High-specification contemporary concrete, through use of white Portland Cement, stone and marble dust, specially selected aggregates, non-fading pigments and a range of finishing techniques – shot blasting, needle-gunning, hand-picking, timber shuttering – can mimic noble materials such as limestone, marble and costly stone finishes like rustication, or create their own vivid, decorative, one-off effects.

Gypsum

GYPSUM, OR CALCIUM SULPHATE, is a softish, natural rock found all over the world. We know it as the raw material of interior plaster, which may be pink, white or grey, depending on purity, since colouring in gypsum is due to mineral or clay traces in the rock bed. When water is added to gypsum and well mixed, the squidgy mass begins to stiffen after only fifteen minutes or so, one reason why plastering is such stressful work.

Gypsum – the word derives from the Greek *gypsos* meaning chalk or plaster – is the most important natural cementitious material other than lime. Its use is thought to have antedated lime, since the temperatures needed to burn, or calcine gypsum are considerably lower: lime kilns devoured scarce fuel. Gypsum plasters are not as resistant to weather as lime renders, but in hot climates they may have proved adequate for exteriors, especially if these were protected by overhanging eaves.

Gypsum plaster 'sets up' differently from lime. The crushed rock contains the fetchingly named waters of crystallization, which are driven off during calcining. When water is added, the reverse chemical action takes place, converting the soft mass back into gypsum. Some moisture will always remain in plastered walls, one reason why they are demonstrably effective in delaying

Details from typical 'new age' concretes.
Top right: Blitzcrete by John Outram, using chunks of brick and other materials in a white cement/concrete. *Centre right*: A standard pale concrete mix with gravel type aggregate, ground and etched to show the texture. *Bottom right*: A highly-textured effect, achieved by using concrete mixed with pebble aggregate. *Inset*: A small detail from a recent award-winning building for St John's College Oxford by MacCormac/Jamieson/Pritchard shows how noble a modern concrete can look when made from white cement/aggregates, and hand-finished to resemble rusticated limestone.

house fire. It was after the Fire of London in 1666 that plastered walls were generally adopted in Britain.

Decoratively speaking, some of the most interesting work with gypsum plasters was done in Islamic countries. The intricate, pierced decoration surrounding windows and courtyards in the Alhambra Palace at Granada, Spain, is one famous example. How this seemingly fragile material has managed to survive more than a thousand years in good shape is perhaps less of a mystery when one reads of the lengthy, elaborate processes that went into Indian plasterwork of a later date. The Indians used shell lime (made from calcinating seashells) rather than gypsum as their cementitious material, but their methods and additives are fascinating, and it seems not impossible that the Moorish plasterers imitated their work to give their gypsum the smooth polish and durability of marble.

The Indian plasterers' recipes included the use of sugared water, egg whites, curds and whey, polishing with a smooth pebble, and even the sprinkling of damp plaster with ground glass, for sparkle. Strange as many of these plasterers' tricks may appear to us, it may be timely, given the burgeoning of interest in this ancient, temperamental material among young designers, to recognize that as far as the creative potential of gypsum plaster is concerned, the late twentieth century has a lot of lost ground to make up.

Compo

ROBERT ADAM (1728-92), who seems to have been as active an entrepreneur as he was a designer, is said to have purchased the recipe for compo, or composition, from a Swiss

Right: Knole, in Kent, is one of England's oldest and most intact ancestral homes, country seat since the sixteenth century of the Earls of Dorset. The splendid plaster frieze and strapwork ceiling shown here are the work of Richard Duggan, later in date than Hardwick Hall.

Below: A detail of the wonderfully vigorous plasterwork frieze in the High Great Chamber at Hardwick Hall, Derbyshire, built in the late sixteenth century. The frieze, in low relief, shows forest and hunting scenes, and retains some of its original painted colouring.

pastor called Liardot. It must have struck him immediately that this impressionable substance, as pliable as putty when fresh from the mould but hardening to an almost stone-like toughness, would be ideally suited to the light, filigree ornament which he had admired and drawn in the excavated ruins of ancient Rome. Instead of being carved by hand, the urns, rams' heads, garlands and bands of ornament which decorated wooden chimneypieces, furniture or picture frames in an Adam interior, could be turned out as rapidly and crisply as coins straight from the mint, saving both time and money. Compo did not look like wood in its unadorned state, but painted or gilded it could pass for the hand-carved item. Glued in place and suitably finished, compo gave a handsomely detailed effect, was light and virtually indestructible. Anyone who has stripped an eighteenth-century chimneypiece to find pine dressed up with compo can vouch for this.

Compo is still used today by specialist plastering firms, in much the same way that it was in Adam's day, often using the identical designs. They usually keep a stock of cast ornament on hand, softening it with a spell in the steamer before applying it.

Above: Samples of contemporary Italian marmorino showing the pure, delicate colours that can be achieved using the 'dust' from working and grinding coloured marbles as both aggregate and pigment in a marmorino finish. The surface is perfectly smooth but not shiny.

Plaster of Paris

PLASTER OF PARIS is probably best known as the white, rapid-setting, rigid material used to make supportive plaster casts around broken limbs. It is, in fact, a form of ordinary gypsum plaster, in which the crushed raw material (calcium sulphate), containing waters of crystallization, is heated at 170 degrees centigrade for about two hours, during which time only three-quarters of the waters are driven off. After subsequent grinding, the product is known in the trade as Class A, semi-hydrate plaster, or plaster of Paris. The retention of twenty-five per cent of the waters of crystallization is significant because it ensures that the plaster sets to a hard, fine-grained mass without shrinking or losing volume – that is, the setting occurs before all the water has evaporated. This explains why the plaster is used for casting, where

shrinking would otherwise spoil the product; and why plaster of Paris casts take so long, often weeks, to dry out completely. Good plaster of Paris is recognized by its weight and its colour: once dry, a cast is quite light and its surface flawlessly white.

In the Middle Ages, the largest known deposit of calcium sulphate was in Montmartre, Paris, whence it derived its name, retained to this day despite the fact that the largest gypsum mining operations are now in the U.S.A. One of the medieval uses for plaster of Paris was as the main ingredient of an extra hard gesso suited to low-relief decoration, because it could be tooled and carved more successfully than the standard softer gesso made from whiting or chalk. As Cennino Cennini describes in his celebrated craftsman's handbook *Il libro dell'arte*, the plaster was first slaked under water 'to drive all the heat from it', then dried into 'loaves' and mixed with an extra strong parchment glue or size. This conscientious preparation – Cennini recommends a month of slaking, modern writers a mere twenty-four hours – resulted in an inert, white material for which he finds the nicely descriptive adjective 'silky'.

There is not enough evidence to establish whether or not this rarefied variant of gesso performed well enough to justify the pains that went into its making, although this was a period when craftsmen seem to have been exceptionally knowledgeable about, and sensitive to, the humblest materials of their trade. Anyone prepared today to investigate Cennini's formula might be pleasantly surprised. The addition of glue size retards setting, something Cennini would have known empirically. My guess is that the special gesso which this process yielded was hard enough to carve cleanly, but plastic enough to apply readily.

Above: A 'stucco lustro' ceiling from Castel-vecchio. Carlo Scarpa's brilliant reconstruction of a medieval fortress in Verona, Italy. Scarpa was a pioneer in rediscovering ancient Italian plastering techniques, of which this dazzling ceiling, coloured with cobalt, is a typical and brilliant example.

Plaster of Paris is widely used today for casting both architectural mouldings and purely decorative objects. For mouldings, it is usually strengthened with a backing of scrim (loosely woven hessian or burlap). This fulfils the same function as bandages do to a medical plaster cast, combining with the plaster to give a little necessary resilience to an essentially brittle material, without adding weight.

Stucco

THE STUCCOIST (FROM THE ITALIAN, *stuccatore*, plasterer) is the acknowledged master of his trade, standing in relation to the ordinary plasterer rather as a master chef does to a good, plain cook. He is primed with special recipes for achieving a variety of high-specification finishes such as tinted, polished, waxed or marbled plaster surfaces. Some of these he will have learned through apprenticeship to another maestro, others, closely guarded, he will have stumbled on by good luck or worked out through experiment. Usually, such is the predominance of Italy in everything to do with decorative plasterwork, from Roman times, he will be Italian. These days his work is in great demand, but being necessarily expensive, clients tend to be super-rich individuals or seriously funded banks, multi-national corporations and the like. Their reasons for choosing marmorino or stucco lustro, to name two of the possible finishes on offer, may range from long-term strategy (these are exceptionally durable, low-maintenance surfaces) to the frank enjoyment of conspicuous consumption.

Curiously, however, the current fashion for high specification stuccoed finishes has done little to clarify the mystery, or mystique, which has grown up around this most exacting branch of the plastering trade. The understandable reticence of the stuccoists themselves is, of course, partly responsible, but the mystery goes deeper than that. Researching the subject, one finds a semantic confusion that should keep specialist writers happy for years.

Architectural historians tend to use the word stucco to denote an exceptionally hard, durable, fine-textured plaster render for exterior finishes. This probably stems from the late eighteenth-century fashion for such surfaces, usually imitating coursed or rusticated stone, said to have been introduced to Britain by Robert Adam on his return from Italy. The stuccoing formulae that interested Adam, however, had a base in traditional practice reaching back thousands of years, beyond Classical Rome to the Greeks and Ancient Egyptians, even to Minoan Crete. But it was the Romans who developed and refined the craft of stucco along with all the other uses of such surfacing materials as lime, gypsum, marble dust and others. Technically, Roman stuccoing has never been surpassed, often consisting of as many as twelve successive coats of increasingly fine textured lime-based renders, finishing up with slaked lime and marble dust worked with trowels and spatulas to give glassy smooth, hard, compacted surfaces.

The Romans already understood, it appears, that to survive in exposed or demanding situations, the comparatively simple lime render plasters of their predecessors – loosely called stucco by many writers on the subject – required additives of one sort or another, and thus laid the foundations for the specialized skills and trade secrets of generations of Italian

Right: A close-up of painted, moulded and carved plaster work from Knole, Kent, gives some idea of the vigour and colourfulness of old carved and painted stucco.

craftsmen. Italian pre-eminence in this field is repeatedly demonstrated over the centuries. It was Italian *stuccatori* who travelled Europe in the seventeenth and eighteenth centuries, when the fashion for elaborately modelled interior plasterwork on walls and ceilings was at its height, executing commissions in palaces and great houses and doubtless passing on information to native apprentices. Interior stucco was different, but equally demanding of specialist knowledge. These *stuccatori* were virtually sculptors, working often in three dimensions as well as bas-relief, and the extraordinary variety of work they left behind, from the frolicking cherubs at Clandon Park, Surrey, to the exquisite ceiling showing Dionysus and Ceres at Moor Park, Hertfordshire, testifies to their technical as well as artistic skills.

Italians also continued using and developing their more conventional plastering techniques, on the lines of marmorino and stucco lustro, though these went in and out of fashion according to the taste of the period. The recipes used in this book are taken from a late nineteenth-century work, recently re-published in Italian, purporting to be a correspondence between two *stuccatori*, one a maestro and the other his earnest and grateful disciple. As one might expect, the recipes offer broad guidelines rather than detailed procedures, but the difficulties that arose in interpreting them may as well be due to the maestro's shorthand instructions to his already proficient pupil as to a proprietorial wish to keep some ingredients or tricks to himself.

It is only right to add that the current interest in the whole family of interior stucco finishes has much to do with the free-ranging imagination of one of Italy's most admired post-War architects, Carlo Scarpa. Had Scarpa not fastened on these traditional skills in the 1950s and 60s to enrich and embellish his highly idiosyncratic and 'modern' works (the Banco di Verona and the Castelvecchio, also in Verona), which exploit the contrast between textures old and new – shuttered concrete, marble, stainless steel, stucco lustro – in a highly sophisticated and cost-regardless way, it seems possible that an extraordinary body of detailed and local wisdom and trade practice might have been lost to us today.

Scagliola

THE OXFORD ENGLISH DICTIONARY describes scagliola cursorily as 'plasterwork of Italian origin, designed to imitate certain kinds of stone'. This hardly does justice to a fascinating technique, undoubtedly an off-shoot of traditional Italian plastering skills, that can produce a finished material with the appearance and many of the properties of natural marble, but with some decided advantages: lower cost, relative lightness of material (for cladding, for example), and total command of the colouring of the resulting *faux marbre*.

Left: London's venerable Reform Club, the early nineteenth-century masterpiece of architect Charles Barry, has some of the best examples of scagliola used on an architectural scale, as cladding for walls and columns in imitation of real marble. Aside from economy, 'scag' has the advantages of colour control, lightness and flexibility. One master plasterer could work on site, if necessary, delivering panels made to precise specifications in any colour combination chosen by the architect. Here classic 'siena' and 'carrara' finishes are shown lining the main staircase.

Right: Individually treated 'pats' of plaster are squidged and kneaded into the base colour of a scagliola mix to create typical marbly swirls and veins. When this has been thoroughly mixed, the whole plaster mass is cut into strips, laid criss-cross on top of each other before re-mixing and kneading to distribute colours as evenly as possible.

Scagliola is made from wet plaster of Paris with dry pigments added, which is worked as a dough and then pressed into a mould and finally sanded, oiled and waxed to give a surface with a   marble-like variegation of colour and a dense, smooth, polished texture that only the alert eye can distinguish from the real thing.

Although the technique is thought to have been used by the Ancient Egyptians, scagliola appears to have entered the more recent building scene around the mid-eighteenth century. Sanssouci, Frederick the Great of Prussia's enchanting summer residence at Potsdam, near Berlin, has whole galleries surfaced with this elegant imitation of real marble. At about the same time, Robert Adam used scagliola for astonishing and intricate floors, such as those in the Trophy Room at Syon House, near London, and for cladding columns and walls. By the late nineteenth century, the advantages of scagliola were so widely recognized that it was routinely used to add a touch of palatial grandeur and opulence to public buildings of one sort or another – opera houses, banks, the headquarters of learned societies, gentlemen's clubs, grand hotels. It would be fascinating to know just how many of the pompous pillared foyers of late Victorian buildings made use of scagliola as cladding rather than real marble. The test, for anyone interested, is tactile rather than visual. Scagliola feels less cool and dense than real marble, and when tapped it sounds more resonant, as it is usually applied over a core of some more hollow material, such as timber or cast iron. Yet in the right situation, scagliola has undoubtedly passed the test of time, and where the material has given way – crumbled or degraded – it is easier and cheaper to employ a scagliola expert to repair the damage *in situ* than it would be to replace real marble with patches.

What has first interested a new generation of artist/craftspersons in this old by-product of plastering skills is the freedom of colours and effects which it offers. In addition, raw materials are cheap, working time concise, and the material adapts to particular requirements, such as a table-top of specific dimensions and colouring.

Modern practitioners describe making scagliola as much like making dough for bread or wedging clay for ceramics. The raw materials are plaster of Paris, dry pigment and water. Having made up a base material of plaster of Paris and water, you sprinkle in dry pigment in the required colours, then knead the 'dough', breaking it open now and then to check the dispersion of pigments. When this is satisfactory, you press the still wet and pliable plaster (which will remain so for about forty-five minutes) into a form or mould and leave it to set long enough to become rigid. For economy and speed of manufacture, the scagliola is sometimes backed and levelled up with ordinary plaster to the required thickness. Either way, when turned out and left to dry naturally, which may take three weeks to a month, the moulded slab presents a smooth, marble-like variegation of colour, swirly or streaky. This needs only the final attentions of rubbing back, oiling and waxing to resemble very closely a naturally occurring marble.

Below: Pietre dure began as virtuoso inlaid work, usually, as here, on tabletops, as here, using a range of marbles and semi-precious stones, like lapis and malachite. As well as their costliness, the cutting of these materials to fit precisely into an elaborate *pietre dure* composition must have been time-consuming. Using variously coloured 'scag' pressed into place in a mould must have saved time and effort without loss of *bella figura*, or showiness.

The fascination of scagliola as a material lies in its flexibility in terms of colour, depending on the pigments you add, and an element of unexpectedness about the final results. Compared with the craft as practised by eighteenth-century Italian *stuccatori*, the contemporary approach is technically happy-go-lucky. Often its creators make a natural progression from working in ceramics (agate-ware is a ceramic equivalent of scagliola). But the commercial and aesthetic success of these inventive craftspersons, working from instinct rather than rules, seems to suggest that working successfully with these ancient materials is very much a matter of determination, vision and readiness to experiment creatively.

Gesso

GESSO IS AN ANCIENT SURFACING material used by artists, gilders and other craftsmen to provide a smooth, fine-textured, white ground for painting in different media and for gilding. It was known by the Ancient Egyptians, who used gesso both as a base for wall painting and as a coating for wooden artefacts intended for decorative painting or the application of gold leaf. Egyptian gesso was made from gypsum, a hydrated form of calcium sulphate, found there in rock and crystal form. Paint colours of great purity were made by using glue size or tempera – made from animal gelatine or natural gums – to bind powdered pigments. Applied to the reflective gesso base, Egyptian painting acquired the fresh and brilliant colouring which remains striking even after several thousand years. By the time Cennino Cennini wrote *Il libro dell'arte* in the early fifteenth century, gesso had become yet another of the sophisticated plastering techniques for which Italians are celebrated. Their expertise gave the technique its Italian name, and those of its derivatives – *gesso grosso* (thick or fat gesso)

and *gesso sottile* (thin or subtle gesso). Essentially, gesso is something between a liquid plaster and thick paint. It is made from the same materials as soft distemper, although gypsum (plaster of Paris) was traditionally preferred to chalk or whiting because of its hardness, fineness and opacity. The ingredients, then, are animal glue as binder, whiting or plaster of Paris for body, and water. Gesso differs from distemper in the relative proportions of the ingredients used and in the way it is made. Artists and gilders are precise about the proportions of size to water, but vague about the quantity of whiting added. *Gesso grosso* has a creamy consistency, whilst *sottile* is more fluid. Both are applied with a brush, in many successive coats, each allowed to dry naturally, and rubbed down to give a smooth, well-compacted surface. Modern practice tends to go for quick results, whereas the old craftsmen exercised patience. Cennini, for instance, recommends that the gypsum for *gesso sottile* be soaked in a bucket for a month, stirred up every day 'so that it practically rots away, and every ray of heat goes out of it, and it will come out as soft as silk'. The hard, fine surface provided by gypsum or plaster of Paris meant that many coats of this soft gesso could be applied without requiring lengthy scraping back to produce fine carved detail.

The sequence of steps in applying gesso depends on the nature and condition of the foundation material. Wood and canvas are primed first with one or two coats of size alone to give a 'thirsty' surface. Rough textured wood is given one or two coats of thick gesso to level the surface, a standard practice still for picture frames and furniture. The gesso should dry naturally – as Cennini says 'this sizing and gessoing calls for dry and windy weather' – but not completely. The best adhesion results from re-coating over a layer of gesso still just this side of dry. On this base, usually many further coats of thin gesso are applied, brushing each coat at right angles to the one before for strength and to avoid a build-up of brush-marks. The gesso is kept just warm enough to remain fluid, but not hot, which would risk trapping air bubbles that would 'blow' and spoil the finish. Contemporary experts recommend leaving newly-made gesso to stand for half and hour before use. Because the animal size goes off after a while, gesso is made up in small quantities.

Smoothing, what painters call 'rubbing back', is essential in the later stages of the process. This is carried out on selected late coats of gesso, and can be done only once their surface is hard dry.

Right: With its idiosyncratic use of colour and texture rather than expensive 'bits', this is very recognizably an interior of the 90s, put together with great flair and imagination by a London artist. The astonishing wall finish, soft blurs of colour drifting like clouds, is based on traditional gesso, which she used by the bucketful to 'paint' the walls, brushing it on warm. Onto this, silky thin washes of watercolour were sponged and brushed. The blotting paper texture of gesso soaks up watercolour with mysteriously translucent effect.

Left: An ancient use of gesso, for comparison, used as the priming over wood for painted decoration on an Egyptian sarcophagus, or mummy-case, in the Staatliche Museen Preussischer Kulturbesitz, Berlin. The paint here is probably the simple glue tempera – raw pigment bound with animal size – which the Egyptians used extensively over gesso. The freshness of its colouring, no doubt helped by being sealed away in a tomb for thousands of years, is quite remarkable.

It is only a corner of a cottage
ceiling, but it could almost be a
piece of abstract sculpture, with its
curving planes and cool, chalky
finish. The photograph shows
unusually clearly the lively texture
of limewash over a coarse lime
render.

Slaking Lime

IDEALLY LIMEWASH should be made from mature putty lime which has been sieved and left to slake under water for a year. During this time the substance breaks down more finely, disposing of any tiny residue of caustic lump-lime and becoming more supple and reliable. The best surfaces for the application of a tinted limewash are those which are very porous. The crude test of porosity is to wet a patch of wall. If it darkens noticeably, the surface is porous and limewash will bond with it. Otherwise, where walls have been treated with a non-porous coating, limewashing is only practicable once the coating has been removed.

You will need

■ Lump lime (unslaked powder or quicklime)
■ Metal bucket for slaking ■ Measuring jug
■ Plastic pail ■ Sturdy rubber gloves
■ Protective goggles
■ Mask ■ Metal sieve

1 *All the equipment is laid out in prepartion for slaking putty lime to make limewash. Quicklime is dangerous, caustic stuff, so gloves, goggles and ideally a mask are important. Pigment can be added to the slaked putty lime and mixed in thoroughly.*

3 *The lime reacts chemically to the water, heating up to 45 degrees, steaming and bubbling as the slaking proceeds. Soon it will dramatically convert the contents to a white pasty mixture – putty lime. For best results, this is left to mature for up to a year.*

2 *Water is being added to the lump lime to slake it . Hot water can be used to activate it if it seems slow to react. Their should be a vigorous reaction within thirty seconds or so.*

4 *Sieving the newly slaked putty lime is essential to remove unslaked fragments of limestone, or unslaked nodules of lump lime, which would otherwise give an uneven finish when the wash is eventually applied to the walls.*

Rough Plastering

RENDERING A WALL WITH 'COARSE STUFF', putty lime mixed with coarse sharp sand, will give a fairly flat surface but one with a gritty, crusty texture that tends to spring fine cracks as it dries. This has often sufficed as an exterior finish, especially when coated with a protective limewash. A certain bumpiness will persist, especially where the masonry beneath is itself uneven, as with old rubble walls. On a rubble, or uneven brick, wall, a surprising quantity of 'coarse stuff' is required to achieve something approaching flatness. The coarse stuff we used was 'haired', i.e. mixed mechanically with a small quantity of animal hair to help bind the mixture together. The wall surface we worked on was old, uneven brick, previously limewashed many times. The bricks were well brushed down with a wire brush, to remove as much flaky paint as possible and thoroughly wetted before rendering. The lime render went on quite easily, thanks to its porous base.

You will need

■ Coarse 'haired' lime plaster ■ Board for mixing ■ Hawk ■ Float ■ Garden spray or large brush for wetting the wall

1 *The haired 'coarse stuff', consisting of putty lime mixed with coarse sharp sand in a one to two and a half ratio, is tipped out on a board or flat surface and thoroughly chopped and pressed with a float to disperse lumps and moisture evenly. It rapidly becomes 'buttery' and smoother as this is done, as the binding lime spreads throughout the mix.*

2 *The test of a thoroughly mixed render is that it clings to the plasterer's hawk when turned upside down. To arrive at this a lump of plaster is scooped upon the float and flung at the 'hawk' several times, till it looks smooth and neat as dough.*

3 *The correct way to begin rendering is to present the 'hawk' vertically to the wall surface, slicing off one layer of prepared lime render at a time, as shown here. The wall surface has been previously well wetted by spraying with a hose or garden spray. It should be thoroughly damp, but not dripping wet.*

5 *The process of smacking on, spreading and smoothing out continues from the first rendered patch, extending outwards to cover the whole surface.*

6 *Before rendering over a new area it is helpful to spray it first with a garden spray. A professional works so fast this may not be necessary, but amateurs will find it helpful.*

4 *The first 'slice' of coarse stuff is spread on firmly with the float, working upwards and outwards. Bits may fall off while you are acquiring the knack, but these can be returned to the original mix and re-worked in till smooth. Firm pressure rather exceptional strength is needed.*

A gutsy rough plastered wall finish topped up with limewash gives this very basic but attractive kitchen enormous appeal. The look is organic and free-form, in the particular way this ancient peasant approach makes possible. Shelves, alcoves, work tops, are all integrated into a whole space bonded together by the 'rough icing' finish given by traditional lime plastering. It is a sort of surface 'sculpturing', miles away from 'fitted' units.

Lime Rendering

THE WORD 'RENDER' DENOTES a coating applied over the outside walls of a building to help protect it from bad weather yet give a unified appearance that may also be enhanced with paint. Where a town house of pretensions might require stucco, a vernacular building would be content with a render: fewer coats, less finely worked and often quite coarse textured, but nevertheless protective. Renders made with lime as cement, using a variety of aggregates or extenders – predominantly sharp sand – have a peculiar charm. Lime render is soft-looking and luminous (lime refracts light) with a gentle, powdery appearance, a distinctive bloom. But its serious contribution as a surfacing material is its inherent porosity or breathing quality. This is critical to the survival of old masonry, especially materials like cob and daub. A single coat of render floated over a well wetted surface gives a pleasant gritty creamy colour. A limewash will help keep it in good condition, because lime processes interact beneficently. But a second render coat, using lime with fine sharp sand, yields a smoother surface with a silvery pallor.

You will need

- Coarse, sharp, well-graded river sand
- A finer grade of washed sharp sand, such as silver sand
- Well-slaked putty lime
- A plasterer's hawk plus a board for mixing
- A steel float
- A trowel
- A garden spray filled with clean water
- An old broom

1 *For a first coat, putty lime and coarse sand are mixed in approximate proportions of 1 to 4.*

2 *The putty is trowelled until buttery smooth on a board and worked with sand until evenly coloured and 'plastic'. The aim is to distribute the fine clinging lime to coat sand grains evenly. A pat of render is transferred to the hawk, lifted up on the trowel and smacked back on the hawk until it becomes smooth as dough and adheres when the hawk is turned upside down. The hawk is presented vertically to the work surface and a slice of render removed and applied to a well-dampened wall surface, trowelling upwards and outwards.*

3 *The first coast is well wetted, using a broom, before the application of a second, finer coat. Damping prevents cracking, or segregation, where the fine lime rises to the surface and carbonates as a thin surface layer, inadequately bonded.*

4 *The finer coat of putty lime mixed with silver or other fine sharp sand is applied over the first. This is thinner overall, but is also used to level up the surface. It should be well compacted with a float, dragged upwards at an angle.*

This close-up of the door surround at my house demonstrates the softly textured luminous quality of a lime render finish. This is an unpainted two-coat lime render.

DEALING WITH CRACKS

Cracks tend to occur as the first render coat hardens, though keeping it moist with spraying will help considerably. They may result from uneven absorption by the substrate, inadequate compacting (which requires physical strength) or insufficient mixing. A second finer coat properly applied tends to fill cracks and bond the render more securely, presenting a smooth, fine-grained surface.

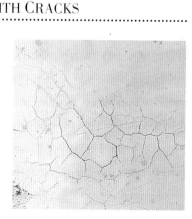

Marmarino Plaster

You will need

■ Putty lime ■ Marble
dust ■ Trowel ■ Hawk
■ Float

A S THE NAME SUGGESTS 'marmorino' is both Italian and related to real marble. Technically, it clearly derives from the ancient practice of combining marble dust – often called marble 'flour' in old textbooks – with putty lime for the final, superlatively fine and smooth coats of plaster, *intonaco*, used to prepare a wall for decoration in *buon fresco*. The pure marmorino finish, in effect a worked, polished, refined stucco, is not exceptionally shiny. It has the smooth low lustre of worn marble. We found it an entirely practicable and achievable plaster finish of great distinction, preferably over small areas of intense interest. Italian plasterers today offer a range of ' marmorino' finishes in which the colouring is supplied by the 'marble dust' itself: Italy is rich in red, yellow and green marbles. We used lime-compatible pigments instead, with more intensely coloured results. All colour samples must be tested beforehand – dried on a board or paper – because lime colours dry much lighter always. Lime-compatible pigments should be mixed in a one-to-one ratio of putty to marble dust (preferably white). One, two or three coats of the coloured *intonaco* must be applied thinly, well compacted and smoothed out with float or spatula, for the best effect. The final 'scraping' gives extra gloss, protection and water-proofing and should not be omitted.

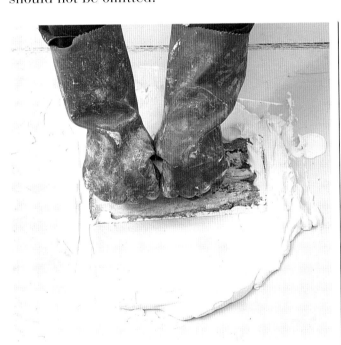

1 *The putty lime, well matured – at least a year is recommended, but old Italian plasterers passed vintage putty lime from generation to generation – is turned out onto a board or clean working space and patiently cut and worked with trowel or float to reach the desired smooth consistency.*

2 *An approximately equal quantity – by volume or weight – of marble dust is gradually mixed into the putty lime. Thorough mixing should disperse the lime and its moisture thoroughly, but if it seems too 'short', not fatty enough to cling, a little limewater (the liquid that collects on top of the putty lime) can be added, and again worked in thoroughly.*

3 *The mixing process of marble dust with putty lime is shown in close up. The 'working' much resembles working flour into a frothy yeast for breadmaking. At first the materials are resistant, the mix 'sullen'. Then, suddenly, the magic happens and the mix coheres satisfactorily.*

4 *The wall surface, in this case a fine-textured plaster mix of putty lime and silver sand (1 putty to 2 silver sand) is given a preliminary wetting with a brush dipped in water or a garden spray.*

5 *The marmorino – marble dust/putty lime mix – is applied very thinly, not more than 4 mm deep, over the existing plaster. It would be better still to apply 2 coats of 2 mm thickness but this may be impractical. The Romans used slave labour after all!*

A close-up of the final polished texture of a simple untinted marmorino. This would have provided a fresco painter with an ideal surface.

Polished and Tinted Stucco

THE POLISHED AND TINTED stucco marmorino, whose application is shown there, follows faithfully a recipe taken from the *Notebooks* of Giacomo Querini di Venezia, first published in 1889 and recently re-published in Italian. We were able to check the ingredients, but not the process, against a contemporaneous recipe. One would expect recipes used by different plasterers to vary somewhat, but these were almost identical. In fact, marmorino itself is not especially mysterious to anyone who has worked with lime. Here we show the application of the final, pigmented marble dust/putty coat, plus the lime/soap mixture The Maestro used to seal the marmorino and add a polishing agent with the soapy liquid. This is a low- rather than high-shine finish, with a beautifully fine, hard, cool, silky texture. Due to the composition of the final marmorino – white lime with white marble dust – I doubt that very deep, intense colours can be achieved without so overloading the mix with pigment as to weaken it. Most critical to a successful finish is achieving a flawless surface, fine coats well compacted, flat as can be: every dimple, dent or irregularity is magnified by the burnishing process.

You will need

- Marble dust (white, from a monumental mason or marble workshop)
- Mature (at least 3 months) putty lime
- Lime-compatible pigment
- Board for working plaster
- Bucket for soap/lime mix
- Pure olive oil soap, 'Savon de Marseille'
- Bain Marie (double boiler)
- Mixing utensils
- Plasterer's steel float and hawk
- Standard brush
- Soft felt or wool rags for polishing
- Gloves and goggles

1 *The putty lime is thoroughly worked on a board until smooth as butter. This is essential to success. In its settled state it is somewhat stiff and lumpy, like cheese curds with a layer of limewater on top. Don't discard this; use a little to lubricate the putty as you mix. The float, forcefully used in various directions, soon works up the necessary smoothness. Twenty to thirty minutes is not too much: large quantities were traditionally beaten with wooden staves.*

2 *The marble dust is mixed in with the putty in proportions of one to one, again until buttery smooth. Our marble dust is light grey: white would have been less distorting to the tinting colour. We used lime-compatible iron oxide red and marigold (orange), dissolving thoroughly in water first. The final colour desired dictates the amount of pigment. Add pigment cautiously, bit by bit, testing colour once mixed on a board. A thin sample, dried in sun or over heat, gives an idea of the final shade.*

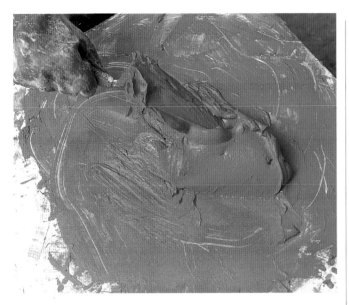

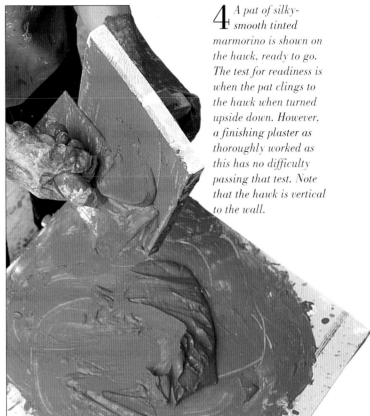

4 A pat of silky-smooth tinted marmorino is shown on the hawk, ready to go. The test for readiness is when the pat clings to the hawk when turned upside down. However, a finishing plaster as thoroughly worked as this has no difficulty passing that test. Note that the hawk is vertical to the wall.

3 More careful mixing and working is needed to disperse the pigment evenly through the marmorino mixture. Tedious though this is, it all helps to refine and make the putty content smoother, more plastic and adhesive. In Italy, plasterers often use coloured marble dust to colour and extend in one operation, cutting one process. However, the colours obtained are decidedly pastel.

5 A slice of the plaster is spread firmly but thinly over the dampened previous coat. Italian plasterers often use steel spatulas for working these final coats, to compact the surface as much as possible, working downwards in fast cross-hatching style. This gives extra-thin layers, and takes years of practice. We found a steel float easier, working across diagonally and then upwards for maximum pressure. The importance of getting a fine, smooth finishing coat cannot be exaggerated. Lime clings beautifully, so bonding is not problem.

6 These are the materials that go into the Maestro's lime/soap coat: a pat of leftover marmarino stucco, plus a bar of pure Savon de Marseille, made with olive oil. This was tracked down at a 'green' cosmetic shop, where it is sold for its purity as a toilet soap. Decorative painters use it for cleaning their best brushes, too, as it has no perfume or chemical ingredients.

8 The melted soap and stucco are combined and left for forty-eight hours. During this time the lime and soap interact to give a frothy-looking surface, while the other ingredients settle out beneath.

7 The soap is being chipped preparatory to melting down. This is done over gentle heat in a double boiler until it liquifies. It must on no account be left too long at this stage. The soap reacting with the lime in the stucco results in a soapy liquid which contains enough oily, waxy substance to add lustre to the marmarino.

9 The froth is scraped off and discarded, leaving a purer mix to be brushed onto the walls. The recipe is not too precise about quantitites of lime in relation to soap here: we used more soap on our second attempt, with better results in the final finish.

10 *The soapy liquid, uncoloured and quite thin, which has settled out on top of a thick sediment of stucco at the bottom of the pan, is decanted into another container, and the sediment is discarded.*

11 *The lime/soap mix is brushed over the dry marmorino. The first coat is brushed on vertically, the second applied when the first is dry, horizontally. The surface must be entirely covered each time. It can be seen here how dramatically the marmorino has lightened on drying, from blood red to a deep coral pink.*

12 *This detail of our first attempt at marmorino shows clearly how tiny surface irregularities, no more than stretch marks, are emphasized by the final soaping and polishing up. Just out of interest, we experimented with heat, passing a blow-torch flame (turned low) and a heated flat-iron across the finish. The torch made no difference; the flat-iron left scorch marks.*

Coral marmarino, as good as we can get it. The lengthy polishing was done with soft woollen cloths, gradually bringing up a deep lustre, shinier than our Italian samples. A beautiful, tactile, durable finish; but one demanding skill and patience.

Making Gesso

GESSO IS AN ANCIENT surfacing material used by artists, gilders and other craftsmen to provide a smooth, fine-textured, white ground for painting in different media and for gilding. It was known by the Ancient Egyptians, who used gesso both as a base for wall painting and as a coating for wooden artefacts intended for decorative painting or the application of gold leaf. Egyptian gesso was made from gypsum found there in rock and crystal form. Paint colours of great brilliance and durability were made by using glue size – made from animal gelatine or natural gums – or tempera to bind powdered pigments. Here we show how to apply gesso to a mirror frame as a base for gilding.

You will need

■ Rabbit skin glue granules ■ Artist's-quality whiting ■ Metal pan ■ Heat-proof container for gesso which fits in the pan ■ Measuring jug ■ Spoon for stirring ■ Sieve ■ Standard brush for applying gesso ■ Silicone or wet-and-dry paper

1 *The gesso equipment laid out ready.*

3 *Next, this mixture in its bowl is placed over just simmering water in the metal pan and stirred from time to time, until melted and liquid. This is the basic gesso 'stock'. It must not boil, or the gesso is weakened.*

2 *The first step is to tip a cupful of rabbit skin glue granules into a bowl, adding water to just cover. This is left to 'fatten', preferably overnight, until the granules soak up water and become fluffy and swollen.*

4 *Whiting is gradually dribbled into the hot stock, stirring gently but thoroughly to break up any lumps. Continue until the stock will hold no more whiting in suspension, that is, it begins instead to settle on the bottom. As an added precaution against lumpiness, the gesso mixture is sieved into a clean vessel (right).*

5 *The wooden frame has been prepared by being given a coat of diluted 'stock' and left to dry.*

6 *Water is added to the gesso mixture, – three parts water to two parts gesso – and well stirred. The gesso grosso is brushed over the frame. When almost dry, more coats of gesso sottile (made by diluting with two more parts of water) are applied. Five or six are needed for a smooth finish, rubbed down with silicone or wet-and-dry paper between the coats.*

Gesso appears in many guises in these pictures of a London artists' workshop – *gesso sottile* brushed over the white wall surface, *gesso grosso* and *sottile* as a base for paint and gilding on the baroque picture frame, and both gessos once again providing a smooth base for further decorative painting on a round table.

Casting a Plaster Moulding

THE PRINCIPLE BEHIND casting is discussed in Chapter 4; briefly, a 'positive' (the shape to be reproduced) is surrounded with a liquid, impressible material (formerly wax, then gelatine, nowadays a hot silicone rubber mix) which, on cooling, can be separated from the 'positive' to leave a 'negative' that can be used to cast with runny plaster of Paris over and over again. But what happens when the positive, as in these pictures, is beyond re-use? The celebrated London fibrous plaster firm who demonstrate here simply build an identical positive from scratch. This is a sculptural undertaking in which skilled plasterers use measurements, but also hand and eye, to make an accurate positive.

The equipment and skills needed to cast an elaborate moulding like this are beyond the reach of the amateur. But we show the sequence to demonstrate the stages involved; the same principles apply to taking much simpler casts.

1 *The replacement positive is created on a wooden backing, for strength, using plaster of Paris with a layer of loose-weave hessian. The boards are fixed with shellac.*

2 *The positive is laid in its trough (above) and closed in by a lid and end pieces of fibrous plaster (left). In other words, a 'sealed' container is created for the mould-making process, which uses melted silicone solution, hot.*

3 *To secure the container rigidly, ribbons of scrim bandages dipped in plaster are draped, wet, across the casket and nailed down both sides to prevent wobbling and distortion during the mould-making.*

4 *Through holes punched in the plaster 'lid', funnels are inserted at regular intervals. These act as conduits for the hot, liquid silicone rubber mould-making material. This is heated in a thermostatically controlled machine, to the correct temperature and consistency – amateurs have to rely on thermometers.*

5 *The hot, liquid, silicone rubber solution is poured slowly and carefully through the funnels. As this cools and hardens it picks up astonishingly fine detail from the positive.*

6 *After the hardening-off time, the funnels, lid and scrim bandages are removed and a perfect mould of silicone rubber is peeled away .*

The storerooms of a firm such as this, constantly asked to supply or re-make replacement historic fibrous plaster mouldings for use in listed buildings undergoing restoration, or simply to install a suitable period cornice in an old house for a private client, are as atmospheric as old attics. The walls are stacked layers deep in moulds, casts, as well as sample boards covered with compo casts moulded from original eighteenth-century ornament, in much the same way as above, though compo is a trickier material and expensive, since carved boxwood moulds are needed to produce perfect replicas.

Casting Plaster Shells

HERE IS A FAMOUS OLD stone building in the Spanish university town of Salamanca where the walls are carved in relief with scallop shells spaced on a regular grid. Scallop shells were the emblem of the religious pilgrim, so it seems likely the building was originally used as a guest-house for those making the pilgrimage to Santiago de Compostela. The image of this fine but severely plain building embossed with the shells, their compact curves picked out by sunlight, stayed with me as both decorative and dignified. I thought it would be interesting to copy the effect using cast plaster scallops attached to a lime plastered surface. Scallop shells are available from any good fishmonger, and casting them is delightfully simple. The effect was fine, left white, the precise scallops contrasted with the pale, sandy textured plaster, but for interest we tried lime-washing them to resemble stone, using raw sienna and burnt umber for tinting.

You will need

■ Shells ■ Liquid silicone rubber solution ■ Clay ■ Sandpaper ■ Plaster of Paris ■ Scalpel ■ Putty lime and silver sand ■ Water sprayer ■ Limewash and pigment

3 *Prepare a basic hard plaster of Paris solution and slowly pour it into the mould. Try to prepare the minimum amount of plaster needed and use as quickly as possible as it will begin to harden fairly quickly*

1 *As with casting cameos (see page 154), a silicone rubber solution produces an accurate, reusable mould of a shell. In this case we found that a liquid solution gave the best result. Place the shell onto a clay base and surround with an impermeable clay wall. Prepare the silicone according to the instructions then pour over the shell until it is completely covered.*

2 *When the mould is completely dry (this may take 12-24 hours depending on the type of solution and the room temperature), carefully remove the shell from its mould. We used two shells of different sizes and so made two separate moulds.*

4 *Leave the cast to dry for 2-3 hours until the plaster feels cold and hard to the touch, then carefully separate it from the mould. Check the cast for any faults, trim off any excess pieces of plaster with a scalpel and rub down any lumps with a piece of sandpaper. Next plan and mark the areas on the wall where the shells are to be placed.*

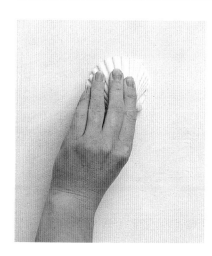

5 *The wall we used had been plastered with a putty lime and silver sand mixture, so we used the same mixture to stick the casts to the wall. Liberally spray the wall and soak the shell cast with water, then trowel a small amount of the putty mixture onto the back of the cast.*

6 *Press the cast firmly into the wall and scrape away any excess putty. Using your finger, smooth a little of the plaster mixture around the edge of the cast ensuring that there are no gaps or air bubbles. Finally, use a damp cloth to tidy up any splashes of plaster from the wall and the casts.*

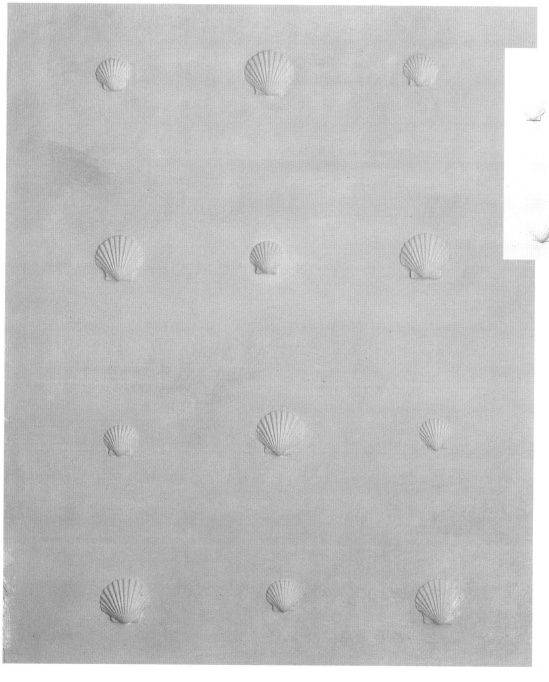

The plain white shell finish is shown here next to the limewashed 'stone'. Scallop shells are an ideal subject for casting, because of their charming shape, but one can imagine many other decoratively-shaped natural objects suited to casting: ammonites, sea-horses, starfish, walnuts halved. And there is a wealth of architectural ornament to draw on. Lime render makes a beautiful background, but a new gypsum plaster would also look good, and can be limewashed too.

A Concrete Clock

THE SOPHISTICATED NEW-LOOK concrete mixes and finishes developed by architects over the past decade have now infiltrated the design scene. The range of clocks, lamps, table tops and other decorative objects made by a young London design partnership, McCollin Bryan, illustrate brilliantly what this once decried, functional material is capable of when given imaginative tweaking. Using white Portland cement and silver sand, and casting procedures amateurs might (with due care) copy, they produce items of classic elegance and simplicity.

You will need

■ Plaster of Paris or potters' clay for making a 'model' or positive mould ■ Vynamould rubber casting solution ■ White Portland cement ■ Silver sand ■ Rubber kidney ■ Steel picture hook ■ Clock mechanism

1 *A sloppy liquid mix of white Portland cement and silver sand is poured into the mould and pressed by hand into all the crevices (above). Shaking the mould levels out the concrete to a flat surface (left).*

3 *With a 'rubber kidney', a potter's shaping tool, Don begins shaping the back, hollowing it out from the centre towards the rim. A clock mechanism and battery must fit in here.*

4 *A steel picture hook mounted on a small metal tab is inserted for hanging the clock. Don uses a kitchen knife, slips in the tab, then pats and smooths wet concrete over the tab, so that the hook alone protrudes.*

2 *A thicker mix – approximately one part cement to three of silver sand – is pressed down in handfuls over the layer of sloppy cement and sand, to cover evenly.*

5 *The newly-cast clock is left to harden for approximately 24 hours. After it is turned out of the mould, it is hung up to cure for a week or two, before being assembled and decoration applied.*

Everything in this picture is made from concrete, plaster or scagliola. The clock is white cast concrete; the obelisk is a lapis blue scagliola; and the table-top is white concrete with an inset piece of plaster photo-printed with classical motifs.

Applied Surfaces

Although an applied surface can be as briskly functional as melamine (resin applied over lowly chipboard) the most interesting ones, explored in this section, are partly or primarily used for decorative purposes. One could argue that tiles and pebble mosaic came about for practical reasons in the first place. But to me the fascinating thing about these ancient surfacings is the fact that simple practicality was never enough. Another powerful human instinct was also at work, bent on introducing order, pattern and beauty into the process. This is creativity. It takes much longer to form a pattern, even a simple geometric design, from heaps of differently coloured pebbles than to roll out the random cobbled areas found in so many cities today. The pebbles have to be sorted by size, shape and colour, a design must be worked out and its outlines marked and followed rigorously, working *in situ*. But the satisfaction of watching the pattern grow under one's hands, connecting spaces in an entirely new way, giving a new dignity to a Roman villa or a Greek Island lane, must have been of a different, superior order, even when you were just one of the many workers employed to carry out the job. Pattern-making, for me, comes into the category of 'serious play', which I believe is one of the most undervalued sources of simple happiness there for the taking.

THE PROFOUND PLEASURE TO BE FOUND in pattern-making, however modest, is one of the discoveries we made while carrying out the various projects in this section. None are too demanding. Most use cheap materials, but the satisfaction quotient they deliver today, as they have for centuries past, is immeasurable.

Mosaic

THE APPEAL OF MOSAIC, to a growing number of enthusiasts, stems from the immense pleasure there is in making something real, solid and handsome from fragmentary or insignificant materials like tesserae, broken china or pebbles. Creating order from chaos is strangely healing. Recent technology has made this ancient surfacing newly commercial, by means of computerized colour selection and modern adhesives. Thus a maintenance-free and permanent mosaic-lined bathroom costs little more than one faced with tiles, stainless steel or etched glass.

Mosaic has always combined function with beauty; utility may have taken priority but an aesthetic intention was there from the start. Its earliest known use – the 'cone' mosaic of 4000 BC in Ur, Southern Iraq – served simultaneously to strengthen and embellish the mud walls of important buildings. Pegs of fired, coloured earthenware were driven into the still plastic mud to make bands of bold, geometric pattern.

The Romans, with their practical genius, developed mosaic made of tesserae – from the Latin *tessera* or 'cube' – which could be cut from marble or stone on site. They discovered that tesserae mosaic, bedded in lime mortar, made smooth, durable pavements to walk on which were not only handsome but also highly practical. That so many Roman mosaic pavements have survived, in North Africa and Europe, testifies to their skilled workmanship.

To this day, mosaicists use Roman terms for the different types of mosaic work. *Opus tesselatum* is the simplest type, where cubes are laid in regular rows on a grid, or staggered, as in brickwork. *Opus vermiculatum* is more expressive: here the lines of mosaic follow the main shapes and outlines, giving visual flow and emphasis to the design. Often areas of *vermiculatum* on figures and other main features were offset by a background of *tesselatum*.

Opus sectile, showiest of all, was a sort of marquetry combining tesserae with cut, shaped sections of marble and coloured stones. *Sectile* is thought to have inspired Florentine *intarsia*, an elaborate marquetry in coloured

Right: This magnificent, severe head of Christ from a ceiling mosaic in a Greek monastery on Mount Horas shows how delicately and finely portraits were worked in comparison to the larger, cruder *smalti* and tesserae treatment used for robes and drapery. *Opus vermiculatum* has been used for the face and a more regular spacing of mosaic, verging on *tesselatum*, for the remainder.

Below: Fish have always been a favourite subject for mosaicist, for their lively shapes as well as their symbolic charge. Here an ancient version shows two fish mysteriously hooked on the same line, and neatly packed into an oval frame. This is just a vivid detail, fishily accurate, from a much larger mosaic floor in the Vatican.

Right: A contemporary fish design pebble mosaic is here being made for inclusion in a garden design scheme. The appeal of fish as a decorative motif persists from Roman times to the present day.

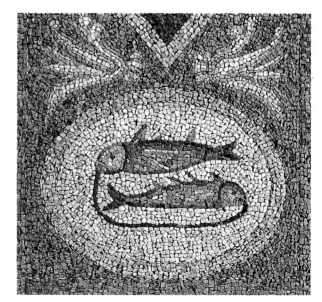

woods, which became fashionable during the late Renaissance. Its influence remains in the splendid scagliola pavement in the Trophy Room of Syon House.

In Classical times, mosaic was almost exclusively used for floors. Its use as a wall covering begins with the introduction of Christianity in about AD 400 as official religion throughout the Roman Empire. Wall mosaics depicting Biblical scenes lined the walls of early Christian churches, most famously in Ravenna in the fifth-century Basilicas of S. Vitale and S. Apollinare. Here beauty, as a gorgeous affirmation of the new faith, takes precedence over function. The change of emphasis is underlined by the introduction of *smalti* (the word comes from the Italian *smalto*, enamel) – brilliantly coloured glass cubes – used profusely to heighten and dramatize the Ravenna mosaics. Gold and silver *smalti*, made then and now to a secret formula, give these masterpieces a jewelled appearance.

Five hundred years later, the Byzantine period signalled a new flowering of mosaic as covering for both walls and floors. In wall mosaic the *smalti* were set into lime plaster, giving a surface which was less even but one which was more refractive. This may have come about by chance, but it seems then to have been adopted for its additional brilliance and now appears a characteristic of Byzantine mosaic. Mosaic pavements usually accompanied wall mosaic, their design developed from the Roman *opus sectile* and often incorporating discs sliced from antique columns and segments of rare marble or porphyry taken from

Later Roman mosaicists, working for a sophisticated clientele, enjoyed showing off their mastery of the craft in such demanding techniques as *trompe-l'oeil*. A whole series of mosaic pavements, generically known as 'debris' or 'remains of the feast', record the sort of litter one might have expected to find, and clear up, after a typical Roman dinner party, mostly fishy – bones, lobster or crab legs, empty shells. But there is a grape stalk or two, what looks like a bay leaf, and sundry mysterious items.

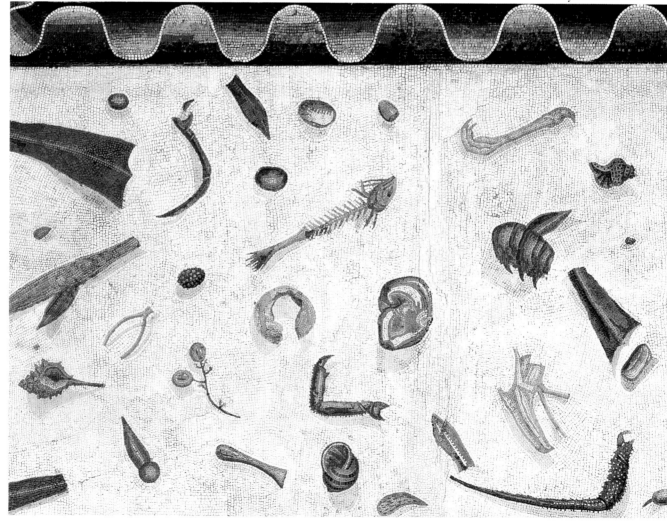

ancient buildings – an early example of architectural salvage.

Prior to the Reformation, a variant of mosaic *cosmati* work (named after a family of celebrated artisans working in twelfth-century Rome) spread from Italy to the rest of Europe, including Britain. *Cosmati* work was made up with much smaller mosaic pieces, usually glass *smalti* but sometimes tesserae of precious marbles, alabaster, *verde antico*, porphyry and malachite. The firmness of *cosmati* made it suitable for covering items of church furniture such as thrones, pulpits, altars and tombs, as well as pavements. Edward the Confessor's shrine in Westminster Abbey was once resplendent in a *cosmati* raiment of coloured marbles.

Mosaic has been in and out of fashion since, enjoying a brief revival at a more utilitarian level for durable flooring for shop doorsteps and the front paths of terraced houses in the late nineteenth century. These nineteenth-century examples appear to have been composed off site, using a straightforward process whereby tesserae, usually black and white, are laid out and glued to a cloth or cardboard backing which is then reversed onto a lime-rendered surface, pressed down, and grouted after the mortar has hardened, after which the backing is soaked off. To the artist mosaicist, this fast and efficient mosaic prefabrication lacks variety. In mosaic terms, this is mass-production.

A detail from a Roman mosaic floor in the Imperial Palace in Sicily showing a hunting party in full cry. A hunter lights a sacrificial fire below the image of Artemis. One tends to think of mosaic as static and formal, but this lively scene, full of movement, barely restrained billowing cloaks and excited animals, shows how dynamic the medium can be.

However, this approach is largely responsible for the renewed interest in mosaic today. There is increasing demand for mosaic by the yard, generally *tesselatum*, to create an ideally practical, durable, waterproof surfacing for bathrooms, splashbacks, shop and restaurant floors. To contemporary eyes the effect, however regimented, has the added value of all hand-made work: it is the antithesis of impersonal vinyl, melamine and the like. Artists and craftspeople also appear to benefit from the commercial revival of mosaic. Their creations, both *in situ* and off-site pre-fabrications, are in considerable demand. Underlining the creative, as against functional, possibilities of this surfacing, they tend to adopt a much looser use of materials, incorporating found objects such as shells, pebbles and even ceramic insulators into boldly executed designs, with a three-dimensional, bas-relief effect which has moved a long way from the earliest functional application of this ancient craft.

Pebble Mosaic

ALTHOUGH THE ROMANS SOMETIMES combined natural pebbles with tesserae in their mosaics, on the whole pebble mosaic developed along different lines, becoming part of a vernacular craft tradition and used almost exclusively for surfacing roads, public spaces, courtyards and gardens – anywhere a tough, cheap, durable paving material was needed. The earliest known example, from Gordium in Asia Minor and dating from the eighth century BC, consists of a simple chequered pattern. Pebbled surfaces are not the most comfortable to walk on – harder on the feet than tesserae – but a properly laid pebble mosaic paving is exceptionally durable, because walking on them drives the pebbles further in.

Pebbles, fragments of stone rounded by friction and weathering, come in many colours. The Greeks and Chinese both enjoyed the subtle tonalities of mosaic made up of a restricted colour range. The Chinese in particular responded to the contrasts in texture possible with pebbles, setting areas of flat brown angular pebbles next to slim, black, shiny pebbles or smooth, white, egg-shaped ones, creating a sort of outdoor carpet against which massive water-sculpted rocks stand out with added drama.

Around the Mediterranean pebble mosaic paving favoured bold geometric repeat designs executed in contrasting colours, usually black and white. The earliest use of pebble mosaic of this kind was Islamic, the Koran's prohibition against figurative representation encouraging more abstract designs. All the paths in the Moorish paradise garden of the Alhambra in Granada, Spain, are pebbled in black and white in scrolls, rosettes, diamonds – a rigorous foil to the exuberant overflow of plant life on all sides.

Not all pebble work is formal and grand. Pebbles are so common, heaped along river banks and shingle beaches, that it would be strange if the notion of using them as a cheap source of hard paving had not occurred to ordinary folk concerned more with practicality than aesthetics. Unpretentious pebbled yards and paths add their tidy texture to farms, inns and private homes all over Britain, echoing on a smaller scale the cobbled (cobbles are a larger edition of pebbles) streets of so many old towns and villages.

Pebblework is currently coming back into fashion as a durable and intriguing surfacing for outdoor spaces, both public and private. Urban back gardens, too shaded for grass, are enlivened by black-and-white pebblework 'carpets' inset as a central feature in stone paving. Pebblework on a public scale, using a colour range of unusual richness, often set

Right: The vivid tin glazes and geometric designs characteristic of early Islamic tiles are resplendent in this detail of tiling in Marrakesh, Morocco. Note the sobering contrast of black tiles framing sections of brilliant colour. The grouting is modest, conspicuous by its absence here, a fine fillet of lime render enclosing each tile securely but almost invisibly.

Left: A somewhat patchwork assemblage of ancient tiles in a looser floral/geometric style surrounds a gateway in the Palais d'Orient, Tunis. Individually beautiful and complex, the tiles have a look of 'salvage' about them, randomly assembled and crudely grouted with what looks like modern cement.

in pre-cast elements for rapid installation on site, is being pioneered in the north-west of Britain by artist Maggie Howarth. She travels all over the country in search of pebbles of a particular shade or mottled colouring, familiarizing herself with local geology in her hunt for useful oddities – red cherts, tweedy granites, pink-veined quartz. Special finds include 'eyes' – white pebbles with a dark spot or holed stones like petrified sponge. With these she composes wildlife pebble mosaics of startling verisimilitude, the earth shades of native pebbles matching to a whisker the russet or tawny fur and feathers of native fauna.

Everyone enjoys collecting special pebbles, striped, spotted, or whatever. It's a holiday pastime not likely to denude a shingle bank. But an extensive project (into which your specials can be set like jewels) needs tons of pebbles, for which you must apply to licensed suppliers. An appealing recent project was an invitation to friends of a noted food historian to bring to his party seventy choice pebbles as a corresponding birthday offering, to be set into a garden path – a thrifty as well as charming idea, rather like the friendship quilts of the American mid-West.

Left: Panels of tiling set into a carved stone or stucco surround make a fairy tale – shades of the illustrative style of Edmund Dulac of the early twentieth century – portal of the gateway to Sitori-i-Makhi Khasa in Bukhara, Uzbekistan.

Far left: Samples of Moorish tiles demonstrate both the complexity and the astonishingly modern-looking simplicity that are typical of Islamic design.

Tiles

THE WORD TILE DERIVES from the French *tuile* and originally from the Latin *tegula*, which almost certainly referred to a roof tile: neither the Greeks nor the Romans seem to have used wall tiles, although the Romans made special floor tiles to lay over their hypocaust heating systems.

Tiles, like other pottery, are made from clay, which is sticky soil formed by the decomposition of feldspathic rocks such as granite. Its chemical description is hydrated silicate of aluminium. Potters' clay is found at various depths and is divided into two types – primary clay, such as kaolin or china clay; and secondary, the common red clay found all over the world and used to make pottery since earliest times. Primary clays are usually white and contain fewer impurities, whilst secondary clays are more plastic and easier to work. The characteristic which makes clay suitable for pottery is its viscosity and malleability when mixed with water, and its ability to harden and retain its shape when dried. Unbaked clay eventually disintegrates. Firing clay at varying temperatures makes it permanently hard, yet it remains to some extent porous, which is why baked clay floor tiles need to be sealed. Coating clay with a vitreous glaze, that is, a thin coating of glass, makes it waterproof and imparts a decorative, shiny surface which can be coloured.

The Chinese were the first to glaze pottery, using both lead and alkaline glazes long before the discovery spread to the rest of the world. Lead glaze was in use in China around

the third century BC and the Romans introduced it to Europe. Lead glaze is transparent, but can be coloured. Adding iron gives a yellow or brown glaze, cobalt blue, copper green and manganese purple or brown. Adding tin to a lead glaze renders it opaque, a discovery thought to have originated in Persia in the ninth century. Tin glaze gave more scope to applied decoration on pottery of all kinds, including tiles, and Islamic potters exploited these with brilliant results, developing the use of lustre as well as underglaze colours. These techniques circulated gradually through the Islamic world, eventually reaching Europe via Spain during the Moorish occupation of Andalusia. The Alhambra Palace in Granada is a dazzling example of decorative tilework, with room after room lined shoulder or waist high with intricate, geometric patterns in brilliant colours. Islamic architectural tilework such as this, along with examples from the more important mosques, has never been surpassed.

Decorated tiles were rarely used in the rest of Europe at this time, and then almost exclusively as a floor covering, usually in churches. Cistercian monks were the main tile-makers in Britain in the thirteenth century, working out of kilns attached to their abbeys. They developed the technique of 'encaustic' tile-making, where designs were impressed into tiled surfaces by means of a wooden die, the hollows then filled in with white clay. When the infill had dried, the surface was scraped clean to leave the white design in sharp contrast against the red clay body. The tiles were then coated with powdered lead ore, which produced a transparent yellow glaze when fired. These encaustic tiles were much harder-wearing than simple glazed tiles. Some of the finest examples of Cistercian tiling can be seen in Ely Cathedral in East Anglia.

In the mid-seventeenth century, the Dutch town of Delft became an important centre for tin-glazed earthenware, and tiles in particular. Though their earlier wares were modelled on the brightly coloured majolica tin-glazed pottery made in Italy, their real success came with the blue-and-white glazed pottery imitating Chinese blue-and-white porcelain imported by the Dutch East India Company. Glazed earthenware was crude compared with the finer bone china or porcelain, but the Delft painters developed their own lively, sketchy decorative style and Delft blue-and-white tiles became almost mandatory as fireplace sur-rounds during the eighteenth century.

Tiles became fashionable once again for both walls and floors during the latter part of the nineteenth century. William de Morgan, who worked for Morris & Co., designed magnificent decorated tiles in rich

The random excitement of brilliantly patterned tiles, broken (deliberately) and recombined in a crazy patchwork, mixing different scales, patterns and designs with extraordinary effect, is displayed in this detail form the Parc Güell, Barcelona, one of the most eccentric and personal inventions of the most celebrated of Spanish architects, Antoni Gaudí, whose work in Barcelona dates from the early decades of this century.

Somewhere between tile and mosaic, a rampageous concrete newt (or lizard) encrusted with fragmented tiles rears out of a tile pool. Another detail from Gaudí's Parc Güell.

colours, including lustre, clearly inspired by Islamic work   centuries earlier. The home of the fashionable painter Lord Leighton in west London contains tiled rooms with pools and fountains inspired by a romantic interpretation of Islamic hammams which created a stir in London society. More prosaically, potteries like Maws and Minton in the Potteries area around Stoke-on-Trent in England manufactured encaustic tiles for hallways and front paths, whose exceptional wearing qualities can still be observed in suburban terraced homes in London today. Rescued from beneath decaying linoleum and shabby carpeting, these are lovingly re-instated and restored as original period features. The grandest examples of encaustic can be seen at Osborne House, Queen Victoria's summer retreat on the Isle of Wight.

Today, the choice of tiles is almost bewildering in its variety, all the way from mass-produced ranges (cheap and practical, if characterless) through expensive reproductions of classic designs from all periods, to handmade, fired clay floor tiles from Mexico and reclaimed antique tiles, coveted for patchwork effects in bathrooms and kitchens. The perennial virtues of tiles as wall or floor covering – waterproof, easy to clean, hygienic, durable – are as attractive today as they have ever been. Even more so, since tiling has become a do-it-yourself activity, made easier by ready-to-use adhesives and grouting packaged in squeezy applicators. But fashion tiling has its own problems: for every homemaker deeply torn between handmade Mexican or reclaimed French, there are half a dozen urgently seeking advice on how to blot out, cover over and generally lose whole walls of tiling that has gone out of fashion and which they have unwillingly inherited.

Right: A detail of the fire surround shown in the large picture.

Above: The tender pastel shades and varied forms of seashells speak for themselves in this charming, mirror-backed sconce, designed by Diana Reynell. Although of recent design, this is very much in the rococo spirit.

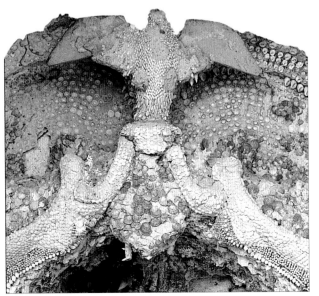

Left: A shellwork crest surmounts the Shell House doorway. Like knapped flints, the shells were all originally bedded in a fine lime render or cement, but at a later date some restoration was done using standard Portland cement mortar.

Shellwork

SEASHELLS, IN THEIR teeming variety of shape and colouring, have provided inspiration to designers and material for craftsmen for centuries. As early as the thirteenth century, Chinese lacquerists were inlaying their pieces with mother-of-pearl. Shells bedded into lime cement lined the grottoes of Italian Renaissance gardens such as the Boboli in Florence, the Villa Madama in Rome and the Palazzo del Te in Mantua. And shells massed with tufa, knapped flint or crystal stalactites were an essential decorative element in the shell rooms, shell houses, bath-houses, grottoes, caves and other garden follies that dotted the grounds of grand, or aspiring, European country houses of the eighteenth century. This was the heyday of rococo with its spiralling, convoluted forms and assymetries which delighted in seashells, both as motifs and as material for encrusting walls, whimsical furnishings like those shown here, and for smaller objects such as boxes and frames, to which deftly applied shellwork confections lent a fragile charm. Whilst the more ambitious projects – the Duchess of Richmond's Shell House at Goodwood is considered the masterpiece – must have employed teams of workmen, shellwork on a smaller scale was taken up enthusiastically by amateurs like the gifted Mrs Delaney, friend of Dean Swift, royal protegée, superlative embroideress. In her old age, the tireless Mrs Delaney moved on to découpage, creating botanical studies

The shellwork fire surround shown below is a faithful copy of the lost original, based on an old black-and-white photograph. Diana Reynell ciscovered that eighteenth-century shell workers used crushed brown bottle glass, pressed into putty, to imitate sand. She makes putty from whiting and linseed oil worked together with a secret ingredient – raw sugar, jaggery, has been suggested – to delay hardening and prevent cracking.

Above: The patient elaboration of this shellwork frame suggests an early and amateur piece. Tiny shimmering shells are packed close as beads or sequins. Shellwork shown here is from the National Trust's Shell House in Hatfield Forest, Essex.

of great beauty and accuracy out of coloured paper, which are now one of the minor attractions of the British Museum. One can imagine the future botanical artist taking pleasure in composing the rosettes of tiny pink shells, which look like moss roses and are such a pretty feature of eighteenth-century shellwork. The refinement and delicacy of the smaller shellwork pieces, and the time and patience needed to cover surfaces with shells no bigger than an orange pip, suggest a feminine hand at work, and one with time to fill.

Contemporary shellwork, currently in great demand, harks back to this miniaturist style. Restorers like Diana Reynell, who works frequently for the National Trust in Britain, collect shells all round the world, bedding them into lime plaster or her own home-made putty. Varnish, which makes tourist souvenirs look like peanut brittle, is absolutely taboo. Peter Coke, the Norfolk-based artist whose exhibitions of shellwork are a sell-out, advocates a light final coat of baby oil thinned with lighter fluid to bring up the natural colours and impart a subtle sheen.

The Print Room

A DIFFERENT, ARCHITECTURAL, use of découpage (in its widest sense) led to the creation of that most appealing of eighteenth-century decorating ideas, the print room. A print room is created by the simple device of pasting prints onto walls and framing them with engraved borders, to simulate frames. In the more elaborate examples, the prints are linked by swags, or cords, hung from rosettes, rings or bows, and finished with pendant tassels, trailing ribbons or cameos. Variety of size and shape, some thematic coherence, but above all a good eye for convincing arrangement, all make for a successful print room. This was early understood. Horace Walpole, that most observant dilettante, records one such at Wanstead, seat of the Childe banking family near London: 'We entered a breakfast room, elegant indeed, prints pasted on buff paper with engraved borders, all displayed in a manner which shows great taste.' The Duchess of Northumberland writes in her diary of others: '...a Hall fitted up with prints on a straw coloured ground', and a 'very good Dining Room fitted up with Prints on yellow paper'. Print rooms were clearly going great guns in the mid-eighteenth century, and their appeal lasted on into the nineteenth, when the Duke of Wellington himself decorated whole rooms in this style.

Professional paperhangers advertised their readiness to make print rooms, but existing examples seem to have been largely the work of family members, enjoying the challenge of 'fitting up' a room in the family seat in fashionable style. Background colours chosen were usually pale – straw, buff, yellow, pink, blue. Prints were collected over years, borders and ornaments bought by the sheet, the work usually undertaken, as Mrs Delaney records, when 'it rained furiously'. There was even an album of print room designs, as yet unpublished, known

as the Wricklemarsh album, now in the Paul Mellon Collection at Yale University, Connecticut. The charm of print rooms has not lost its appeal; in fact, with the photocopier making the use of real period prints unnecessary, there seems to be a commercial and serious revival of this attractive and elegant form of découpage

Découpage

DÉCOUPAGE, FROM THE FRENCH *découper*, to cut out, is understandably undergoing a considerable revival at present, both at hobby and commercial craft levels. Its appeal to both is obvious. It is much easier and quicker and less artistically demanding to cut out and paste down printed images on small or large objects, including walls, than to paint or

Print Rooms were the most architectural development of the genteel craft of découpage. This elegant example, from the National Trust's Blickling Hall in Suffolk, is in fact a stylish but recent re-creation, using the 'straw yellow' background so popular in the eighteenth century, old prints, and modern etceteras – bows, borders – available through National Trust shops. With photocopying, the expense of amassing a collection of genuine old prints is no longer necessary, or desirable. Some judicious 'ageing' (we use instant coffee) makes photocopies quite acceptable. With print room arrangements, symmetry is everything.

stencil similar motifs by hand. The result has a professional chic and completeness which is thrilling to people who freely admit that they don't know one end of a paintbrush from the other. Anyone, the theory runs, from childhood onwards, can cope with scissors, paper and glue, and have fun doing it.

This is true as far as it goes, but to make something seriously appealing and commercially saleable from pasted cut-outs involves taste, patience, craftsmanship and creative thinking. The materials may be universally available in this age of photocopying and laser printing, but as ever it is what you make of them which counts. Professional work is more thoroughly prepared, the base coats patiently smoothed, colours carefully chosen, the cutouts hand coloured for individuality, the finishing coats of varnish sufficient to 'lose' the edges of the cut-outs, with possibly a few expert touches, such as contrast lining, a two-step craquelure varnish for instant ageing, along the way. The more handwork, which the French call *petits soins*, that goes into the piece the more distinguished the effect. Some professionals today make use of short cuts, colour prints from wallpaper or wrapping paper, acrylic resin varnishes to embed the découpage in a thick, clear, shiny coating; but one rapidly tires of these subterfuges. The colour prints are *déjà vu* and the acrylic resin looks plastic.

The best models for an aspiring découpeur, a source of inspiration for colours, groupings, borders and much more, are invariably antique, because this ingenious craft goes back a very long way, even before printing made black-and-white images accessible in the fifiteenth century.

L'arte del povero

THE CHINESE USED CUT-OUTS, not paper ones but embroidered motifs salvaged from precious robes and hangings, to decorate small objects centuries ago. The discovery of

We tend to think of découpage as a fast, pretty way to give a boring object – tray, lamp base – new vitality. But this fancifully decorated painted Venetian commode, marble topped, shows how cunning use of scissors and painted motifs can be used to give an air of rococo fantasy to a high-styled piece of furniture. The inspiration here is eighteenth-century chinoiserie.

printing coincided with the Renaissance fashion for complex wooden inlays, *intarsia*, on wall panels and furniture, and led to the use of printed borders, shaped, glued down and varnished to create a poor man's version of costly inlay. The Italians called this use of découpage *l'arte del povero*, poor man's art, and were quick to exploit its possibilities. When the craze for oriental lacquer swept across Europe, creating a demand for colourful, whimsically decorated painted furniture, Venetian craftsmen became adept at turning out items, large and small, painted, découpaged with hand-coloured prints, and heavily varnished. While these rarely look much like the originals, they are extremely attractive in their own right, with a charm and naivety that makes them collectors' items today. From the variety of motifs used, fashionably dressed figures, bizarre flora and fauna, rococo swirls and classical borders, it seems clear that printers supplied the workshops with special printed sheets of suitable designs in black and white, to be hand-coloured. The quantity and complexity of découpage varied with the price an item might fetch. A grand bureau or commode might be smothered in an elaborate network of motifs, whereas a rustic chest of drawers might have no more than a nosegay on top and a swag on each drawer front.

In the eighteenth century, découpage joined the list of genteel occupations which fashionable women, with time to kill, took up as creative hobbies. In 1762, the *Laidies' Amusement Book* [*sic*], a collection of designs expressly for découpage, was published, and aristocratic ladies from Marie-Antoinette down embarked on découpage projects for decorating fans, boxes, screens, lap desks. Those who could afford to, with lamentable extravagance, went as far as cutting up original prints by masters such as Boucher, Watteau and Fragonard, but, on the credit side, artists like Mrs Delaney formed her exquisite découpage botanical pictures from thin papers which she coloured herself.

'L'arte del povero', or Italian cut paper imitation of old lacquer or eighteenth-century Japan, cuts a great dash in this magnificent Venetian bureau/secretaire, intricately decorated with cartouches and delicate floral motifs, the whole buried under countless coats of varnish, aged to an overall amber tone, aside from the drawer fronts.

Painting and Applying Tiles

THE INSPIRATION FOR THIS project came from a trip to Canberra in Australia, where I discovered that glazing, decorating and firing pottery 'blanks' (shaped pieces, fired once to the biscuit stage) was a popular winter occupation. It struck me as a totally satisfying hobby: you skip all the wedging, shaping and initial firing; on the other hand, your artistry on the decorating side can take over at the finishing stage, much as the ceramic painters (often women) did traditionally in the pottery factories. My Australian friends were tackling whole dinner services!

You will need

■ Biscuit tiles, (blanks) ■ Three ready-made glazes ■ Large softhair brush and two small artist's brushes ■ Spirit level ■ Tile adhesive ■ Tile cutter ■ Tiling grout and comb ■ Cloth

1 The first step is to calculate the number of tiles needed for the project. It is better to over-estimate in case of any mishaps. Then, using a damp sponge, wipe them to remove any dust.

2 Choosing white as our base colour, we found that adding a little water to the glaze made it more workable. Load the brush with glaze and lightly sweep over the tile so the glaze almost pours onto the surface of the tiles.

4 A good tip is to load the brush heavily with glaze, pausing after finishing each tile, and trying not to overpaint, as this causes the glaze to look lumpy. Any mistakes can be gently scratched off later when it is dry. When the glaze has dried (10-15 minutes) apply the next coloured stripe – here a fine green line applied with an artist's brush.

3 We chose a plaid design for our tiles in pale pink and green. The glazes we used remained remarkably true to their original colours after firing, but always choose colours from fired examples of the glazes. Working on blocks of 9-12 tiles at a time, we then used a soft pencil to sketch the design onto the tiles. Then, using a soft brush trimmed to size, we painted on the pink glaze stripes.

5 A kiln and an expert to supervise the firing need to be found – many art colleges and potteries now offer these facilities. The tiles were carefully stacked in tile racks and then fired. The firing temperature relates to the glazes used.

6 Using these racks and firing all the tiles at the same time helped to produce an even finish, but one should allow for some variations in colour. On the whole the colours of the glazes remained true and the fired tiles had a soft shiny appearance.

7 *Divide the surface of the fireplace into sections drawing horizontal and vertical lines to be used as starting points. When working out the gid, keep in mind the gap to be left between tiles for grouting.*

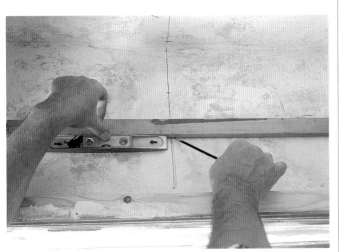

8 *Try to keep the sections small and workable. Use a spirit level and a long ruler or piece of wood to check the lines are straight after finishing. Keep in mind the level of the floor, which may be uneven. And if so adjust the lines to compensate for this.*

9 *Now prepare the tile adhesive. Using a trowel or a spatula, cover one of the sections with a thin layer of adhesive. Apply a thicker layer to compensate for any uneven surfaces. Then, using the comb provided with the grout, score the surface to help the tiles adhere more easily.*

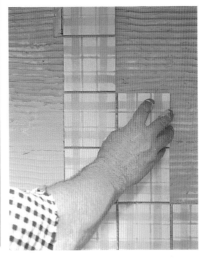

10 *Gently but firmly press the tiles into the adhesive. Small markers can be used to create even gaps between the tiles for grouting but with practice they can be judged by eye. It is helpful to step away from the work occasionally to check on the straightness of the lines.*

CUTTING TILES

Unless one is particularly fortunate it is unlikely that the tiles needed to cover the fireplace will fit exactly. In this case it may be necessary to trim some of the tiles to size, using a tile cutter. Available from tile or hardware shops, it is an essential tool for any tiler. Cutting the tiles takes some skill. The cutter itself is a simple piece of equipment but the method requires some practice. It is a good idea to practise by cutting any imperfect or excess tiles which will not be needed for the actual work in order to build up confidence.

To cover the surface of the fireplace completely it may be necessary to trim some tiles to size. Working on a flat hard surface, balance the cutter against a straight metal edge and firmly score the tile.

Grip the tile with the head of the tile cutter at the point where it has been scored. Then grip the other end of the tile with your hand and press firmly: the tile should break cleanly into two pieces.

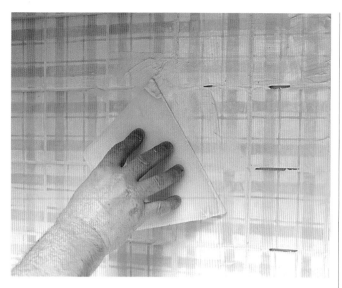

11 *When all the tiles have been applied, the gaps between them then have to be grouted. Specialist tile and hardware shops will be able to advise as to the most suitable type to use. We chose to use a grout in powder form which was mixed to a thick, sticky consistency. Using a spatula the grout is worked firmly into the gaps by wiping it over the tiles.*

12 *Once again it is a good idea to grout small sections at time, pausing occasionally to check on progress. Using a slightly damp cloth, gently wipe over the surface of the tiles to remove any excess grout. After the grout has dried, the final step is to use a clean dry cloth to polish the tiles back to their original sheen.*

Pastel plaid tiles make a really pretty feature of an old fireplace, the pink picking up the wall colour effectively. One of the rewards of decorating one's own tiles is being able to get the colour exactly right for a particular spot. A plaid design is easy to do, and looks very professional.

Tesserae Mosaic Doorstep

ONE OF THE CHARMS of mosaic is its versatility. It can be used on a large or small scale, applied to almost any solid surface and confer the dignity of its ancient materials and satisfying repetitiveness to surfaces better covered up. It is permanent and, best of all, the making and installing of a mosaic is not beyond any neat-fingered person, though the young mosaicists who carried out this project tell me there is an instinctive sense of rhythm and spacing, which some people are born with. We discussed various locations for a mosaic – tabletop, splashback, for example – but settled on a mosaic treatment for my front doorstep, an unlovely chunk of crude concrete. I like mosaic best when it is used structurally, as a practical bathroom surfacing for instance, or as paving, where good looks are subordinate to function. I left the design to Chris and Celia and they chose an inscription based on old Celtic runes, signifying welcome, hospitality and good fortune, though we toyed with the idea of *cave canem* (beware the dog) in the Roman fashion.

You will need

- Brown paper
- Pencil/eraser/ruler
- Brush ■ PVA adhesive ■ Rag
- Clippers or 'snips'
- Small tiles 2 cm square ■ Tile adhesive
- Notched trowel
- Sponge ■ Bucket
- Tile grout ■ Stanley (utility) knife blades ■ Acid cleaner (hydrochloric acid to clean off cement)

1 *A brown paper template is cut to fit the mosaic site exactly (left). The design is drawn in reverse, like mirror writing. The equipment for the task is shown below.*

2 *The design is being worked out in tesserae cut from small tiles (cheaper than pre-cut), and the tiny squares of ceramic glued down individually with PVA onto the paper template. This is absorbing to do, but requires patience.*

3 *The completed mosaic glued onto its backing shown next to the doorstep, which has been extended a few inches to make a better-sized step and give the design more room, using OPC cement and sand packed into a wooden form.*

4 *A coat of tile adhesive is spread evenly over the top, front and sides of the step with the notched trowel, following the maker's instructions. The mosaic is turned over and carefully placed in position, pressing down evenly.*

5 *After the adhesive has dried fast, the brown paper is soaked to peel it away. Then a commercial grout is spread over the whole mosaic, using a trowel, the surplus wiped away with rags and sponge. It is left to harden.*

6 *Some grout invariably remains on the mosaic, as a thin film. Stanley (utility) knife blades are used to scrape off blobs. Then, wearing mask and gloves, hydrochloric acid diluted in 15 parts water is brushed on carefully. When it 'fizzes' it is washed over with lots of clean water, leaving an immaculate mosaic.*

This mosaic on my front doorstep, with its welcoming inscription, has beautifully enlivened the entrance to my house, demonstrating the adaptability of this ancient technique.

Making a Shellwork Frame

L IKE MOST PEOPLE WITH scavenging instincts, I have amassed a good basketful of special shells on holidays by the sea, by now gathering dust. With the ravishing examples of earlier shellwork in mind, it seemed the moment to put my collection to better use. What I had not reckoned on is just how many small shells of an identical sort are needed to make a quietly textured background against which 'specials' stand out with proper emphasis. I happened on a shell version of a bead curtain, grimy and going cheap, in a junk shop. Well washed, these supplied my ground cover. The frame, with its usefully containing border, was to hand. Coral twigs were another beachcombing find.

You will need

- Ready-made frame
- Decorator's caulk
- Selection of shells
- Artist's spatula
- Brass Screws
- Brass picture wire
- Chisel and hammer
- Water-based paint
- Baby oil and lighter fluid ■ Raw umber water-based paint

1 *Basic materials for shellworking are laid out to hand – frame, already base-coated with a matt water-based paint, torpedo applicator for decorator's caulk, shells both ordinary and special (for shape and/or colour) and coral twigs.*

2 *Before embarking on a shellwork project, it is wise to experiment with your materials. A dummy run, without adhesive, shows whether you have enough ground cover, and how to group your colourful special shells to best advantage while at the same time making an interesting composition overall.*

ADHESIVES/GROUTS

It is essential to use a good adhesive for attaching the shells to the frame. Strength is obviously important as well as drying time: you need enough time to work. Colour must also be considered. It is worth sacrificing a few shells to test out several different adhesives, helping you to find the most effective.

Decorator's caulk

Silicone sealant

Gapfilling adhesive

3 *After roughing out the design, the shells are bedded in the white caulk a section at a time. The caulk is squeezed on like icing, then spread quite thinly (2-3mm) with an artist's spatula, and each individual shell is pressed firmly down. I mixed plain and 'tweedy' coloured shells randomly as ground cover.*

4 *The 'composed' elements, featuring special shells, took more time to decide upon. The caulk allows approximately thirty minutes before hardening, so this is no problem. Tweezers are useful for adjusting the lie of a particular shell, or for slipping tiny shells into noticeable gaps.*

5 *Wiring on a coral topknot was trickier. I used brass screws, the smallest available, and brass picture wire, because they are rust proof. The screws were driven in so just their heads projected, making an anchoring for lengths of wire, used to bind the coral in place.*

6 *After securing with wire through the coral's natural holes where possible, grout is squeezed around the twigs for extra stiffening and solidity.*

7 *Picking out one of the more vibrant colours from the shells we decided to liven up the visible parts of the frame. We choose a dilute blueish grey colour paint and wiped it over the frame using a sponge.*

8 *Borrowing a tip from expert Peter Coke I brushed the shells with baby oil and lighter fluid, bringing up their natural colouring while imparting the most delicate lustre. Because the white caulk looked too clinical, I brushed a dilute raw umber paint over the visible plaster interstices.*

To hold pride of place as a dressing table mirror, the frame needed a hinged 'leg' of plywood, secured by a cord and screwed to the frame with more tiny screws. All in all, this is a gratifying way to convert gleanings from family holidays into permanent mementoes.

The final steps are to clean the completed mosaic well, then grout and once again clean thoroughly. It is an especially clever stroke to use flat tiles on curved pots such as these, common earthenware transformed into objects of great fascination and presence, more Gaudí than gaudy.

Patchworked Pots

THE MOST SATISFYING patchwork mosaic is undoubtedly made from flat ceramic pieces, smoothly bedded to give full value to the riotous, informal colour possibilities. Broken tiles are the perfect material, but how do you find enough of them? The solution, according to Spanish architect Antonio Gaudí, is to collect huge numbers of whole tiles in chosen colours and patterns and break them, before re-assembling them in a colourful mosaic. He even had tiles specially made, and the celebrated result is Barcelona's unique Parc Güell, where colours and patchwork shapes flow over rounded seating and surfaces like a surreal herbaceous border. The handsome mosaic pots shown here follow the same principle.

You will need

■ Ceramic/earthenware pots or bowls or flower-pots ■ Pencil/eraser ■ PVA adhesive and brush ■ Tiles – white, glazed and patterned ■ Clippers ■ Tile adhesive and grout ■ Palette knife ■ Sponge/cloths or rags ■ Hammer

1 *Pots are sealed with diluted PVA brushed on and left to dry. The row here includes different shapes and sizes, all curved and substantial but simple in line. Choose solidly made, weighty pieces, without handles or other excrescences.*

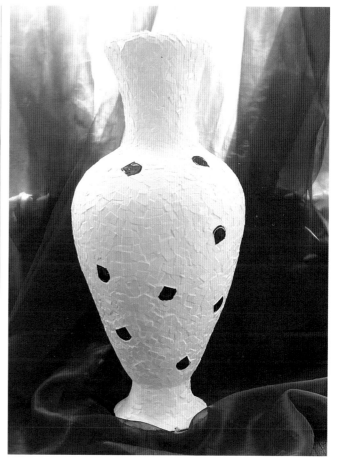

2 *Designs are drawn onto the pot with pencil. Our pots are not a crazy patchwork, but use fragments to create an orderly flow of design and colour, contrasted with white. They look surprisingly Moorish or Chinese as a result: definitely superior.*

3 *The next stage is to smash the tiles. This is best done by laying them between sheets of newspaper before banging away with a hammer, though there is a danger of going too far and reducing them to pieces too fiddly to work with. A strong shape like this seems to call for strong, clear designs, which means a fair number of largish pieces. Clippers were used to snip fragments into smallish, irregular pieces. These are stuck down one by one with tile adhesive, spread with a palette knife.*

Transformation of junk piece into stylish drinks cupboard is complete, with new chromed knobs replacing some of the earlier handles. Two finishing coats of matt polyurethane varnish give resistance to wear and tear. A final option could be to 'antique' the découpage with a water-based *craquelure*, with raw umber oil paint rubbed in to show up the crackle – a common treatment for 1990s découpage.

A Trompe-l'œil Cupboard

T HE GENTLE craft of découpage is revived thanks to the ease with which images can be resized by photocopying. Most découpage, whether commercial or amateur, is small-scale. We liked the idea of pushing the technique on further, in imitation of the Italian designer Fornasetti, whose witty use of graphic images applied to furniture and other decorative objects influenced a generation of fifties designers. The maximum photocopied enlargement was employed. This is *faux* Fornasetti, but a permissible development of the traditional Italian use of pasted-on images to decorate furniture.

You will need

■ Access to a photo-copier
■ A flat-surfaced cabinet ■ Acrylic primer ■ Sandpaper
■ Blackboard black
■ Masking tape
■ Wallpaper paste
■ PVA adhesive

1 *A fifties cabinet, of undistinguished ply, is a suitable subject – plain, flat and inexpensive. We removed the characteristic utility-style handles and secured some loose ply with panel pins and wood adhesive.*

2 *The oak veneer needed thorough priming first to fill the grain and even up the surface. Acrylic primer – the contemporary fast answer to gesso – is fast drying with a useful 'build'. Two coats were applied, enough to fill.*

4 *A plain black interior looked stark by comparison, so we decided to découpage this, too, using a Fornasetti trick of a deliberate change of scale.*

3 *After thorough smoothing with sandpaper, the cupboard was painted inside and out with blackboard black, an inexpensive high-opacity paint which dries matt and is widely available. The photocopies were measured and trimmed, then attached temporarily to the doors and drawer fronts with masking tape to check fit.*

5 *All cut-outs were brushed over with ordinary wallpaper paste on the back, and stuck down carefully using a soft rag to press out air bubbles and stretch and flatten the paper at the same time.*

6 *A re-brushing on top of the découpage with more paste helped to fasten down any loose bits – usually round the outer edges – more securely. Once dry, a coat of PVA adhesive diluted with water was brushed over the decoupage.*

Découpage

ÉCOUPAGE IS AN appealing way of dressing up the sort of functional items – trays, waste bins, lamp bases and shades, desk paraphernalia – one buys because they are useful and cheap rather than attractive. Old battered tin trays, for instance, graduate to the tôle class, given a coat of typical tôle paint colour (black, dark green, red, vivid yellow), an attractive découpage motif, contrast lining and several coats of glossy polyurethane varnish. The items here are in the same class – an old plywood hatbox and waste bin. The restrained chic of black-and-white images against coloured backgrounds seemed appropriate here.

You will need

- Photocopied images
- Craft knife ■ Matt paint ■ Acrylic scumble glaze ■ PVA adhesive
- Polyurethene varnish
- Foam paint applicator
- Water- based 2-part craquelure ■ Burnt umber artist's oil colour

1 *A coat of a buttercup matt paint followed by an orange-tinted acrylic scumble glaze gave the hatbox a vivid yellow finish not unlike the sharp Turner's Yellow popular in Regency England. This is left to dry.*

2 *Architectural images photocopied and enlarged are cut out using a craft knife and a cutting mat. The knife makes cutting fiddly detail easier. Scissors blunt too rapidly.*

4 *To glue cut-outs to the surface some people prefer to use wallpaper paste as this allows the pieces to be moved around but we found that PVA adhesive gives a tougher bond. Smooth the motifs flat with a clean, soft cloth.*

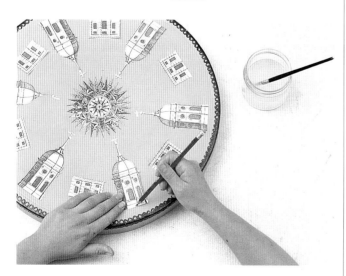

3 *Place the cut-outs onto the lid and move them around, experimenting with different designs. Once the best arrangement of cut-outs is found use a pencil to mark their positions lightly on the hat-box.*

5 *When dry a dilute coat of instant coffee or tea is brushed over to give the motifs a parchment tint. The hat box is finished with three coats of polyurethane varnish to give a tough and durable surface.*

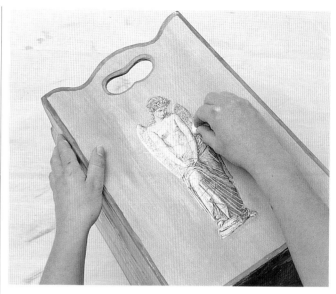

1 *A small foam pad makes edge 'lining' on the waste bin go more smoothly than a brush. The deep blue emulsion paint used to 'dry brush' the bin was used for lining.*

2 *A two-stage craquelure varnish system, water-based, was applied over the découpage motifs only. The classical figures seemed to fit the elongated bin shape best. Dry overnight.*

3 *A fine web of cracks appears in the craquelure surface. These are brought up by rubbing in burnt umber oil colour, then rubbing off to leave colour in cracks only. Varnish well.*

The finished hatbox and waste bin have a great deal more charm than the purely functional. A comparatively simple set of skills transforms them into objects redolent of the graces of the last century, when découpage was an acceptable pastime for ladies with time to spare for decorative pursuits.

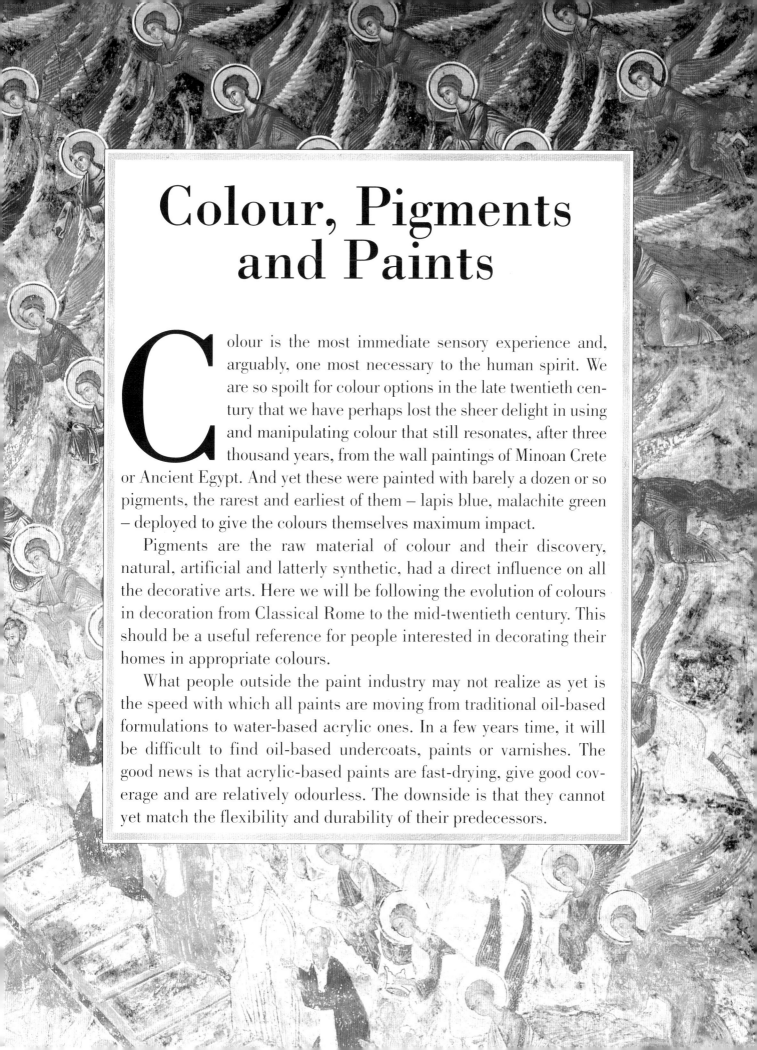

Colour, Pigments and Paints

Colour is the most immediate sensory experience and, arguably, one most necessary to the human spirit. We are so spoilt for colour options in the late twentieth century that we have perhaps lost the sheer delight in using and manipulating colour that still resonates, after three thousand years, from the wall paintings of Minoan Crete or Ancient Egypt. And yet these were painted with barely a dozen or so pigments, the rarest and earliest of them – lapis blue, malachite green – deployed to give the colours themselves maximum impact.

Pigments are the raw material of colour and their discovery, natural, artificial and latterly synthetic, had a direct influence on all the decorative arts. Here we will be following the evolution of colours in decoration from Classical Rome to the mid-twentieth century. This should be a useful reference for people interested in decorating their homes in appropriate colours.

What people outside the paint industry may not realize as yet is the speed with which all paints are moving from traditional oil-based formulations to water-based acrylic ones. In a few years time, it will be difficult to find oil-based undercoats, paints or varnishes. The good news is that acrylic-based paints are fast-drying, give good coverage and are relatively odourless. The downside is that they cannot yet match the flexibility and durability of their predecessors.

Almost forgotten, ancient paints – limewash, soft distemper – are being revived, for aesthetic as well as ecological – no chemicals, no mysterious additives – reasons. In this section the mysteries surrounding these old formulations are described. They were often devised to produce simple, home-made paints. Their charm, a combination of soft texture and clear colour, well justifies the modest effort needed to master an unfamiliar medium.

Buon Fresco

THE FASCINATION OF *BUON FRESCO* – true fresco – lies in the notion of achieving permanence via slender means. Murals in *buon fresco* are painted virtually in watercolour, hence their radiant purity, yet wall paintings at Knossos have survived more than 3000 years. The secret, once again, is lime. In *buon fresco*, dissolved pigment is applied to wet lime plaster. As the lime carbonates and the moisture evaporates, the pigment layer is locked into a fine crystalline layer that forms on the surface of a lime system which is virtually reverting to stone. The absence of any modifying medium delivers the colours in ideal clarity, hence the vividness of such recently cleaned frescoes as Michelangelo's on the ceiling of the Sistine Chapel.

Painting in fresco is notoriously demanding: wet colour dries many shades lighter, transparent pigments lightest of all, so it takes a trained eye to determine the colour values of a completed fresco, which might take weeks to dry. The painter is also working against the drying time of the plaster base, drawing water up out of it to give fluidity to the brushstrokes.

Giorgio Vasari, the sixteenth-century writer, was not exaggerating when he described fresco work as the most challenging – he uses the word *virile* – confronting a painter. Fresco painters, from earliest times, found ways to get round the difficulties. A well-prepared, smooth, white, well-compacted base was essential. The Roman author, Vitruvius, recommended six coats of progressively finer lime plasters, each applied while the previous one was just moist. The penultimate coat, known as the *arriccio*, was usually knocked up from equal quantities of slaked lime and marble dust. On this the painter transferred his cartoon, pouncing pigment through pricked outlines in paper. These were linked into a sketch with a wet brush. The final *intonaco* coat was applied over a section only, the size of a *giornato* (day's work) depending on its complexity. At the day's end the edges of the *giornato* were carefully bevelled off, to allow the next day's plaster to be laid with an invisible join.

Right: A detail from one of the heroic frescoes painted by Mexican artist, Diego Rivera (1886-1957), to re-invent and celebrate his country's Aztec Indian history. Here Indian craftsmen, under the commanding eye of a lordly overseer, are shown mixing colours for the two painters in the foreground, watched by an interested crowd.

Left: Dilapidation often adds a poignant beauty to *buon fresco* painting, as in this fragmentary image of a Madonna, or possibly patron saint, on a wall in Peru. The painting is naive, compared with the great religious frescoes of the Italian *quattrocento*, but the colours are delicious. Due to the lime-restricted palette, one rarely encounters a poor colour in fresco.

Limewash

If you add water to lime putty in the proportions, roughly speaking, of one part putty to two parts water, the result is a milky fluid traditionally known as limewash. It has been used as both an exterior and interior paint all over the world for thousands of years. Limewash is the simplest, purest and in many ways most durable of all the traditional paints currently attracting so much interest. It is also, as are all lime-based products, not a little mysterious. Nothing could be more unlike a conventional paint: instead of a thick substance which needs hard brushing out to spread it evenly and smoothly over a wall surface, limewash is liquid, usually slapped on loosely with a large brush. On the Greek islands, where limewashing is the secret behind the dazzling whiteness that sets tourists snapping excitedly, it is not unusual to see elderly black-clad women tackling the annual limewashing ritual using a little string mop, dipping into a bucket and slopping the stuff over their sugar-cube cottages casually and familiarly.

Part of the fascination of limewash, compared with any other surface finish, is that layer after layer of such a fluid paint can be superimposed without appreciably building up the surface, without risk of adverse reactions between one material and another. Every coat applied improves what is already there, so that white grows more brilliant and colours richer and more complex. Limewash shares in the chemical event – carbonation – central to all lime-based processes in contact with air. Drying, in the sense of feeling dry to the touch, and becoming opaque (limewash is as transparent as water as you apply it) happens quite rapidly, in a few minutes under a Greek sun, but carbonation continues indefinitely. In the process, this infinitesimally fine layer of watery wash reverts to its first chemical state, calcium carbonate or limestone, reactivating and strengthening the underlying lime system – previous limewash coats, lime render, lime mortar – all the while. The strangeness of this to people accustomed to modern solutions, where redecoration means stripping off the old before you can put on something new, needs no underlining. Lime-based processes come across as seductively natural, appropriate and sound. When you add to this discovery the fact that limewash colours are hauntingly beautiful and the texture of the finish powdery soft and matt to the eye (though hard to the touch), it is hardly to be wondered at that lime makes ardent converts today.

The most satisfactory substratum for limewash is

Right: Also typical of the Greek islands is the old practice of limewashing paving as well as walls. White reflects back sunlight, so this tradition may help keep temperatures down, helped by the cool blues and greens often used for doors, furniture, gates and balconies. The slightly caustic nature of the lime is also a deterrent to insects, and mildly antiseptic.

Left: Blinding white against a cobalt sky, this is how limewash, layer upon layer, looks under the Greek summer sun. Colours as chalky but intense as the blue and red alongside can only have come about through repeated coatings of tinted limewash. In Mediterranean countries limewashing is part of the rites of spring; its extraordinary luminosity joined with the dazzle of sea and sun, making such vignettes unforgettable.

a lime render or plaster, the more recently applied the better. Lime on lime provides optimum conditions for success in terms of bonding, durability and colour intensity. Old lime plaster and render, bare or previously limewashed, are also good. Bare gypsum plaster and weathered Portland cement are also suitable; bricks take limewash well but need to be well wetted and require many coats to cover evenly. Breeze blocks are excellent. What these surfaces have in common, in varying degrees, is porosity. The crude test of porosity is to wet a patch of wall: if it darkens noticeably the surface is porous and limewash will bond with it.

Experience shows that limewash gives the best results where the chemistry is right. It must be first choice, on aesthetic and conservationist grounds, for old buildings with suitable substrata. The further you get away from these conditions, the less predictable the outcome.

The limewash itself should be made from mature lime putty which has been sieved and left to slake under water for a year after its initial slaking. During this time the substance breaks down more finely, disposing of any tiny residue of highly-caustic lump-lime remaining, becoming more supple – fatty, buttery to the touch – and stable. Making limewash with immature lime putty runs the risk of these 'fiery particles' blowing or blistering on the wall. Mature lime putty is increasingly available from specialist sources (see List of Suppliers). While the causticity of mature lime is considerably less than that of newly slaked, it is still strong enough to damage sensitive areas such as the mouth and, particularly, the eyes. It is essential to wear protective goggles while making and applying limewash and to guard against absent-mindedly rubbing your eyes or mouth. Rubber household gloves are a sensible protection for the hands.

Even in a state of disrepair, a limewashed exterior has something poetic about it. On his Eastern European farmhouse, it is the colour that scores, the vivid ultramarine blue that cobalt imparts to limewash.

Tinting Limewash

TRADITIONALLY, LIMEWASH was tinted with cheap local earth or mineral colours (hence names like 'Suffolk pink'), which gave a wide range of shades, from brownish-red to tawny ochre yellow. Earth and mineral colours are lime compatible and stable in use. Blue pigments have always presented difficulties. Many, like ultramarine, can be adversely affected by the lime and should be applied directly after mixing. The ideal blue is cobalt, old-fashioned blue-bag-blue, a little bundle of colour dipped into the washing water years ago to make the wash whiter than white.

Pigments used for tinting lime should be pure, without extenders or additives, so powder colours as used by children are not suitable. The chemistry of pigment manufacture is now so advanced that synthetic pigments are more and more common, and it can be tricky identifying their components. As the synthetics are as yet unproven, it is safest to rely on the colours shown on the charts on pages 105-109 as lime compatible, and to buy from a reliable colour merchant. Powder pigments, also called 'dry colour', are all intermixable to create whatever shade is required.

Soft Distemper

WHEN PAINTED ON A WALL, soft distemper looks not unlike limewash – it has a similar chalky bloom and clarity of colour – but it does have a pronounced rustic character of its own. This is a brushy texture, achieved by spreading the dense, pasty substance out over wall surfaces. The old painters went to some trouble to eliminate this brushiness, but in my view it adds to distemper's appeal. It resembles brushed suede, and rooms treated to this velvety finish acquire a soothing serenity and simple charm.

Soft distemper – so called to distinguish it from variants such as oil-bound distemper – is made from chalk or whiting, to give opacity; animal glue size to bind; dry pigment as a tinting agent; and water. All ingredients are soaked individually in measured amounts of water overnight to 'fatten', and then the size is melted in a double boiler, cooled and mixed into the soaked whiting. The dissolved pigment can be added at this stage. Distemper wet

Below: Northern Europe traditionally prefers limewash in warmer colours, vivid under a greyer sky. Ochre yellow, with an orange tinge, is popular. Splendid examples can be seen in Sweden, Denmark, Finland and Russia, usually on grander houses like this Swedish mansion, Treholm, Gard. The ochre was intended to imitate stone

Left: More vivid yellow limewash in a northern setting, this time framing neo-classical stonework in a handsome archway giving onto a huge cobbled yard at the Bishop's Palace, Roskilde, Denmark.

is many shades darker than distemper dry, so tinting requires testing samples on paper and drying them over heat or with a hair-dryer to discover the eventual shade.

One of the advantages of using soft distemper is that it will adhere to most reasonably porous, non-shiny surfaces, such as matt emulsion, lining paper, dry lined walls, all bare plasters or painted brick. It is a breathing paint which, correctly made with the right proportion of a strong size, covers in one coat and will not brush off on clothes – contrary to old wives' tales. Its basic ingredients are cheap and widely available, and it is easy to make at home and straightforward to apply. Prepare walls for distemper with a thin coat of size or wallpaper paste, allowed to dry before the application of the distemper.

Distemper has two main disadvantages as a wall finish: firstly, it is not washable; and secondly, a relatively large quantity of pigment is needed to tint it – three to four times as much as limewash. Another disadvantage is that you cannot paint over it with matt emulsion; this causes the paint to flake off, as many people have found when trying to emulsion paint over old whitewashed ceilings. However, you can easily apply a fresh coat of distemper, as long as successive coats employ a weaker – that is, less of a more dilute – size. In the right situation, a distemper finish will last surprisingly well, with a little touching up from time to time.

Along with limewash, distemper was for centuries, and all over Europe, the cottager's preferred interior paint. In Scandinavia it was still being used until the 1950s, when plastic paints swept the board, and countless old distempered interiors survive there from the nineteenth and even eighteenth centuries, as they do in Italy and eastern Europe. The cost of pigment for tinting seems to have exercised thrifty peasantry, and there exist many references to the use of *ad hoc* colouring matters, from fireplace soot to berry juices and animal blood, as well as local coloured earths or minerals, such as the celebrated 'Falun Rôtt', a by-product of the Kopparberget copper mine in the Swedish province of Dalarna (see page 116). Unlike limewash, which reacts chemically with certain pigments, notably blue, distemper is inert and any fading is usually due to the action of light.

Colourwashing

THIS ANCIENT TECHNIQUE WAS revived by the late John Fowler, one of the more innovative and iconoclastic of British decorators of the inter-War period. His discerning eye for paint effects gave freshness and spontaneity to the formal country house interiors where

he largely worked. Fowler liked colourwashing for bedrooms, where its relative fragility as a coating was less critical. This was the man who coloured picture frames with gouache, liking its airy delicacy, and when a 'fussy housekeeper' wiped his handiwork off with a damp cloth, cheerfully remarked that it could easily be replaced, and did so.

Fowler's colourwashing on soft distemper is a simple, lovely way to intensify a distempered room colour without having to load on pigment. The walls are first coated with soft distemper in a neutral shade – creamy white was the usual choice. Over this a diluted distemper, fluid as milk but tinted more strongly with additional pigment, was slapped on in a loose cross-hatching style, leaving some base colour showing. Once dry, the process was repeated.

Right: Dark oak beams, russet red limewash and washy blue windows make a heartening splash of colour on an old house in a Danish village.

The colourwash looks bizarre while wet because of the intensity of wet distemper, but it dries obligingly to the softest dappled colour imaginable, thanks to the absorbency of the substratum and its pale, reflective colouring. It is a proven expedient for arriving at vivid colour on a soft distemper base.

Egg Tempera

WITH SO MANY PAINT BINDERS to choose from today, it takes a real effort of imagination to think back to a time when painters were bedevilled by the need to 'fix' or attach their colours to a surface for a long time. Whether the artist was painting walls, decorating tombs, illuminating manuscripts, furniture or – rather later – painting alterpieces or icons, the search for reliable binders was pursued almost as seriously as the artistic conception itself. Whether one painted for a living, for the glory of God (or Pharaoh) or to satisfy a creative daemon, the fear that this intensely pondered, worked and lovely thing might powder away, or darken irredeemably, must have been a thorn in the artist's side.

The choices were limited. There was *buon fresco* and glue paint, proven over time, and there was an alchemist's cupboardful of odd ingredients – plant saps and juices, earwax, animal glue, starch, gruel, whey – many of which, however fortuitously discovered, turned out to have a solid scientific justification.

Simplest, and neatest, of natural binders was the contents of an ordinary hen's egg, both yolk and white, together or separately. Egg tempera, egg yolk mixed with dry pigment, gave a smooth, fluid paint, somewhat transparent; 'glair' or egg white made a clear, brittle adhesive medium much used by illuminators. Tempering a pigment, roughly speaking, means mixing the raw colour into a substance that converts it into a workably smooth, flowing paint. Egg yolk, diluted with a little water (distilled is recommended) makes an agreeable, smooth, adhesive, somewhat transparent paint to which body could be added with chalky substances. The outstanding quality of this old, simple paint is its extraordinary toughness, hardening over time to become a film that can withstand most

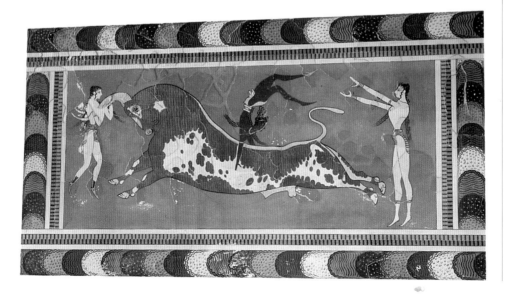

Showing the joyous impact of a quite limited colour palette applied in *buon fresco* on a white stucco base, this mural of Cretan bull-vaulting comes from Knossos. Though over 3000 years old, its state of preservation is extraordinary. Note the intricately detailed though simple-looking border design.

Egg tempera is another medium that survives undiminished and unscathed over the centuries. This elegant *Madonna and Child* by Carlo Crivelli, the fifteenth-century artist, displays the aptitude of this medium for rendering the finest of detail immaculately. If you examine the flesh tones closely you can detect the tiny parallel brushmarks which were used to shade and model in egg tempera. The same use of brushstrokes is used to shape the rosy apples and the deep folds of the Virgin's beautiful mantle stitched with pearls. Egg tempera was used in *buon fresco* painting for fine touches added when the mural had dried – eyelashes, lips, jewels and so on.

chemical attack, while retaining a clarity of colour and freshness that seems little short of miraculous.

Pigments

Pigments are the raw material of paint colour. In contrast to dyestuffs, which are completely soluble, pigments have body, a primary particle which resists the finest grinding. This gives pigments opacity, or covering power, though this varies from one to another and is also affected by the binder or medium used to attach the pigment colour to a surface. Pigments are usually classified according to their composition – whether organic or inorganic – their source – natural or synthetic – or by whether they are white, transparent or coloured. But perhaps the simplest way to grasp a highly complex subject, with endless ramifications, is to see pigments as belonging to three categories: natural, which includes earth and mineral colours; artificial, where, for instance, coloured glass is ground to give Egyptian Blue; and synthetic, where pigments are chemically manufactured to match the colours of existing pigments.

The paint industry today favours synthetic pigments because, produced in controlled conditions, their performance is predictable, their colours are consistent and purer and they have additional advantages, such as resistance to fading and rapid dispersal through a medium. On the other hand, synthetic pigments are often more expensive, and aesthetically there may also be a loss. Paint historians claim that old, hand-ground pigments, with their less regular and finely divided particles, refract more light and give a richer, visibly more satisfying coloured paint surface. The fact that modern synthesized petro-chemical pigments add their quota of pollution to the environment is also a consideration today.

The History of Pigments

The earliest natural palette was limited, by modern standards, though the warmth and naturalness of earthy reds, tawny-ochre yellows, subdued browns and soft grey-greens, sharpened by soot black and lime white, remain as compelling as ever. Egyptian wall paintings strike one as vivid and handsome and in no respect limited in their palette. The Egyptians developed the first artificial pigments, grinding lumps of coloured glass or frit to give blue and green, but they seem to have used these colours sparingly, for well-judged contrast, perhaps because of their high cost. They also used mineral blue and green made by crushing lapis lazuli and malachite: these pigments would have been still rarer and even more costly.

The quest for a cheaper blue persisted down the centuries, not unlike the alchemist's search for the Philosopher's Stone which would turn base metal into gold. It was not fully resolved until 1704, with the invention of the first synthetic pigment, Prussian Blue, named in honour of its inventor, a colourman from Berlin named Diesbach. A deep green-blue, it was made from animal blood and alum. Until then, the rarity and cost of a deep blue had made it a symbol of preciousness, hence the traditional use of this colour for the Virgin's mantle, and also its conspicuous display on the exterior (railings, doors)

Claude Monet's celebrated yellow and blue dining room at his home at Giverny in Normandy must be one of the seminal interiors of this century. Monet planned the colour scheme to show off his important collection of Japanese prints and oriental and other porcelain, almost certainly mixing up the different shades of yellow himself before passing the work on to his painters. Monet gave some time and thought to all the colour schemes in Giverny, mixing and testing out ideas with his foreman. The paint used here would most probably have been a lead-based oil paint which would have lent itself ideally to these spectacular yellows.

and interiors of wealthy households during the eighteenth century.

The development of new pigments over the centuries must have been driven primarily by commercial interests, to satisfy both artistic and decorative needs, these generally shading into each other prior to the Renaissance, when the distinction between artist and craftsman was less formal. But fashion, too, a delight in novelty springing from all sorts of motives, was also a powerful spur to experiment. Glutted with colour as we are now, it requires a real stretch of the imagination to picture the sheer impact of colour itself on a population rationed as to available and affordable shades, let alone the impact of completely new colours – vermilion, orpiment (Turner's yellow), alizarin crimson, pea green, the Victorians' beloved mauve. As each was launched, taken up – first by the top strata of society, then percolating down – it was gossiped about, admired and envied.

Robert Adam gave the already lighter, brighter decorating colours of the mid-eighteenth century a further, influential tweak. Adam spent some time in Rome studying and drawing classical ruins, many then undergoing excavation for the first time, and he returned to Britain with a head full of colour ideas, some based on classical painted

Lime/casein paint made a tough exterior coating for wooden houses like this Laundry and Machine Shop, *circa* 1790 in the Hancock Shaker village in Massachusetts, U.S.A. The Shakers used colour sparingly in interiors and on furniture, but here the 'buttermilk'-type paint would have been permissible as a protective, therefore functional, coating on exposed timberwork.

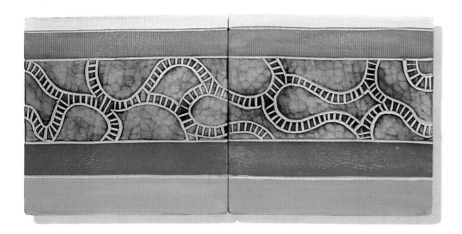

ornament, some no doubt influenced by the sun-washed colouring of contemporary Italy. Making use of the richer palette offered by an advancing paint technology, the young Scots architect introduced bright, clean pinks, blues, lilacs and greens into his interior schemes. Current research indicates that Adam's approach to colour was much bolder, and more complex, than the dreary pastels which came to be known as 'Adam colours' a century or so later would suggest.

Concern for appropriateness when choosing decorating colours for period houses has from conservationists and paint historians to a wider public. People who have seen the restored interiors of public buildings, stately homes or Williamsburg clapboard cottages, tend to be impressed by the convincing way authentic colour schemes executed in the original paints 'hang together'. The result is a growing interest in so-called historic colours, and to a lesser extent traditional paint media. There is no denying that appropriate period colours and paint treatments contribute atmosphere and a feeling of rightness to interiors, whether eighteenth-century, Victorian, Edwardian or Art Deco, and restoring them is a fascinating and rewarding exercise.

A folding mirror by the artist Howard Raybould, created by using several different media including wax, a piece to be touched as well as viewed.

A Historical Decorative Palette

THE COLOUR SWATCHES SHOWN HERE are accurate recreations of paint colours used and available from classical times through to the 1930s. The colours shown in each group do not, of course, represent the full colour range available at any one time, because this would also include all the previously existing colours. The aim is to show, for comparison and interest, colours that are distinctively associated with, and introduced during, the time in question. The reasons for a colour appearing at a particular time are various. Often it signals a new pigment, such as Turner's Patent Yellow, recently recreated in the drawing room of Sir John Soane's house in London, a typically acidic Regency colour, or the mauve which took Victorians by storm after Queen Victoria sported a mauve crinoline at the opening of the Great Exhibition in 1851. Sometimes the reason is more pragmatic, such as the khaki invented during the Indian Mutiny of 1856, when Sir Henry Lumsden noticed that patrol troops whose white uniforms were dusty escaped snipers' bullets more often than those whose uniforms stayed clean.

But the adoption of a 'typical' period colour must always have had as much to do with fashion as with technology. The rage for daring colour combinations – mustard, violet, yellow and blue – that followed the Ballets Russes's performances of *Scheherezade* in 1910, with costumes and decor by Leon Bakst – is a case in point. Another is the fashion for white-on-white decorating schemes in the 1920s, launched by Syrie Maugham's famous drawing room, with white rugs by Marion Dorn, madonna lilies in glass vases, white satin curtains, chairs, sofa, even a white piano. The game was to combine many different shades and textures of white for a glamorous, spectacular, recklessly impractical effect.

Choosing suitable period colours is made easier today by the fact that so many paint companies offer ranges of historic paints, based on the findings of consultants, usually paint historians, experienced in analysing pigments and their vehicles from 'scrapes' and 'cores' from old walls. Some of their recreations have been controversial, like the notorious Germolene Pink re-instated in one Irish stately home by the National Trust. Not everyone is convinced by the Adam 'pea green' in the gallery at Osterley. Such reactions are probably inevitable. Paint colours tend to alter over time, fading, softening, acquiring, in the case of lead paint, a distinctive chalkiness, so restoring an interior to its original colouring, however authentic, sets up shock waves comparable to the brouhaha that attends the cleaning of a celebrated painting or the ceiling of the Sistine Chapel. The colours may be more violent, or sombre, or dreary than we expect. Tastes change, and we also tend to like what we are accustomed to. A welcome way through this dilemma is the increased attention historians and conservationists are now giving to all the other products which can give clues to the colour preferences of past generations. These include fabrics, embroidery, prints, porcelain, all of which, taken together, build up a context of colour references against which a restoration scheme can be tested. Unlike painted surfaces, which inevitably alter and deteriorate, assuming they are not over-painted regularly, these different products may have been preserved intact, a scrap of folded-over fabric retaining all its original brilliance, porcelain still more so. *(Continued on page 109.)*

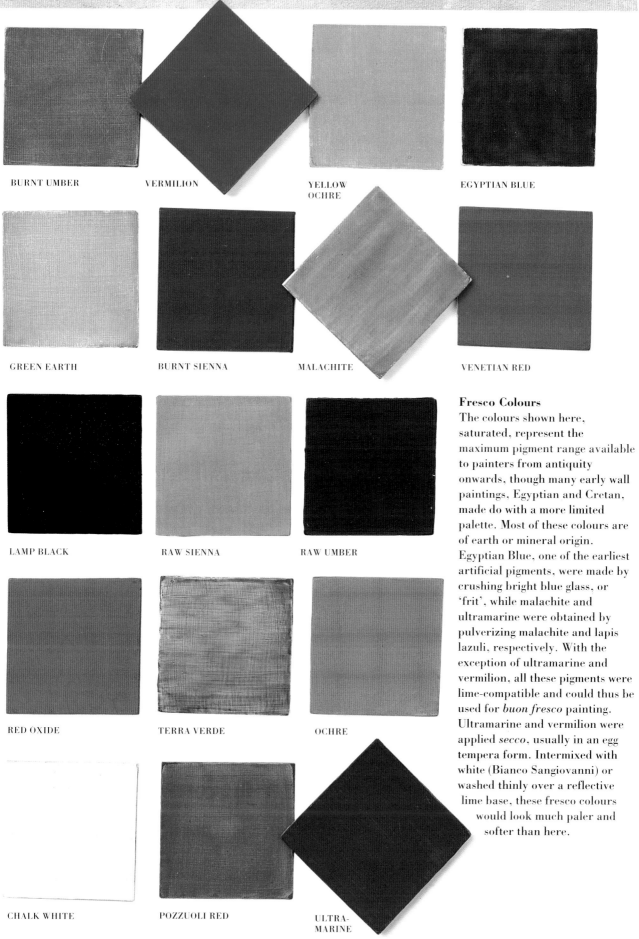

BURNT UMBER

VERMILION

YELLOW OCHRE

EGYPTIAN BLUE

GREEN EARTH

BURNT SIENNA

MALACHITE

VENETIAN RED

LAMP BLACK

RAW SIENNA

RAW UMBER

RED OXIDE

TERRA VERDE

OCHRE

CHALK WHITE

POZZUOLI RED

ULTRA-MARINE

Fresco Colours

The colours shown here, saturated, represent the maximum pigment range available to painters from antiquity onwards, though many early wall paintings, Egyptian and Cretan, made do with a more limited palette. Most of these colours are of earth or mineral origin. Egyptian Blue, one of the earliest artificial pigments, were made by crushing bright blue glass, or 'frit', while malachite and ultramarine were obtained by pulverizing malachite and lapis lazuli, respectively. With the exception of ultramarine and vermilion, all these pigments were lime-compatible and could thus be used for *buon fresco* painting. Ultramarine and vermilion were applied *secco*, usually in an egg tempera form. Intermixed with white (Bianco Sangiovanni) or washed thinly over a reflective lime base, these fresco colours would look much paler and softer than here.

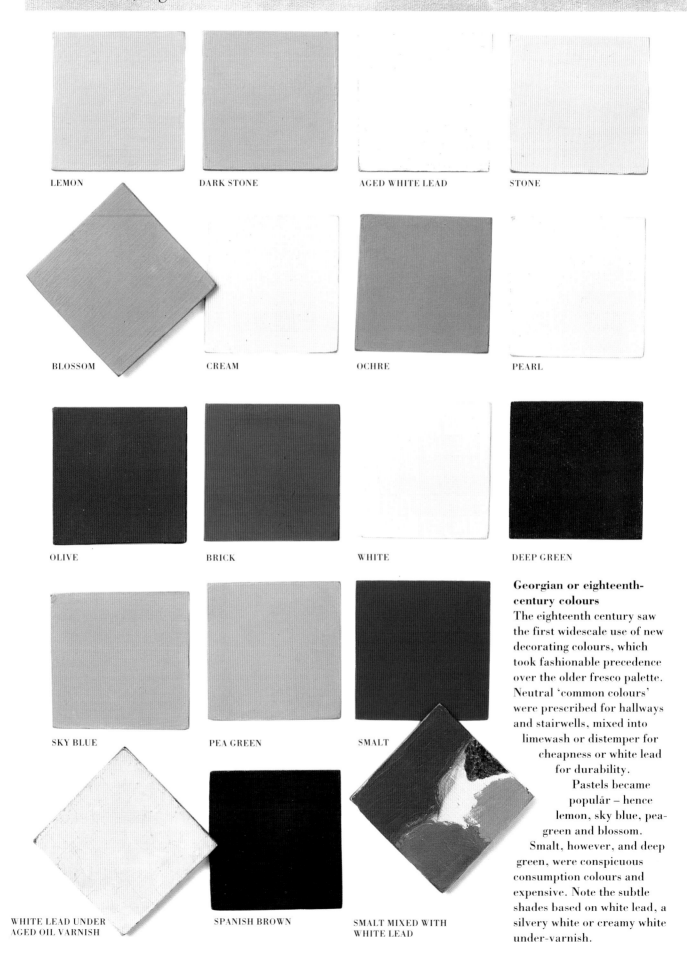

LEMON

DARK STONE

AGED WHITE LEAD

STONE

BLOSSOM

CREAM

OCHRE

PEARL

OLIVE

BRICK

WHITE

DEEP GREEN

SKY BLUE

PEA GREEN

SMALT

WHITE LEAD UNDER
AGED OIL VARNISH

SPANISH BROWN

SMALT MIXED WITH
WHITE LEAD

Georgian or eighteenth-century colours

The eighteenth century saw the first widescale use of new decorating colours, which took fashionable precedence over the older fresco palette. Neutral 'common colours' were prescribed for hallways and stairwells, mixed into limewash or distemper for cheapness or white lead for durability.

Pastels became popular – hence lemon, sky blue, pea-green and blossom. Smalt, however, and deep green, were conspicuous consumption colours and expensive. Note the subtle shades based on white lead, a silvery white or creamy white under-varnish.

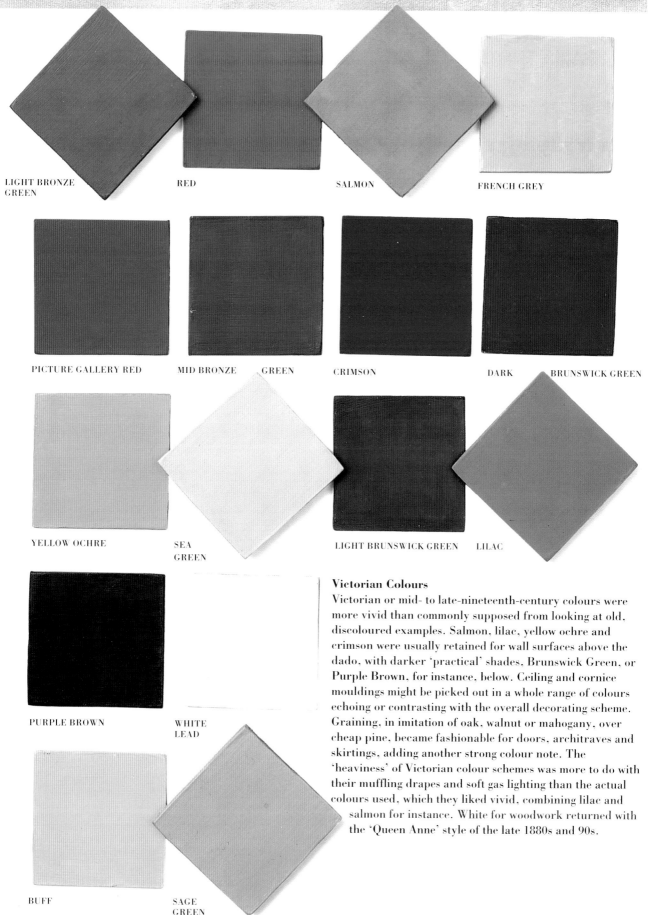

LIGHT BRONZE
GREEN

RED

SALMON

FRENCH GREY

PICTURE GALLERY RED

MID BRONZE   GREEN

CRIMSON

DARK   BRUNSWICK GREEN

YELLOW OCHRE

SEA
GREEN

LIGHT BRUNSWICK GREEN   LILAC

PURPLE BROWN

WHITE
LEAD

BUFF

SAGE
GREEN

Victorian Colours

Victorian or mid- to late-nineteenth-century colours were
more vivid than commonly supposed from looking at old,
discoloured examples. Salmon, lilac, yellow ochre and
crimson were usually retained for wall surfaces above the
dado, with darker 'practical' shades, Brunswick Green, or
Purple Brown, for instance, below. Ceiling and cornice
mouldings might be picked out in a whole range of colours
echoing or contrasting with the overall decorating scheme.
Graining, in imitation of oak, walnut or mahogany, over
cheap pine, became fashionable for doors, architraves and
skirtings, adding another strong colour note. The
'heaviness' of Victorian colour schemes was more to do with
their muffling drapes and soft gas lighting than the actual
colours used, which they liked vivid, combining lilac and
salmon for instance. White for woodwork returned with
the 'Queen Anne' style of the late 1880s and 90s.

PURPLE
BROWN

TURQUOISE
BLUE

PALE CREAM

BRILLIANT GREEN

PRIMROSE

OXFORD BLUE

EAU DE NIL

MIDDLE
BROWN

AZURE

DEEP CREAM

PEACOCK BLUE

SIGNAL
RED

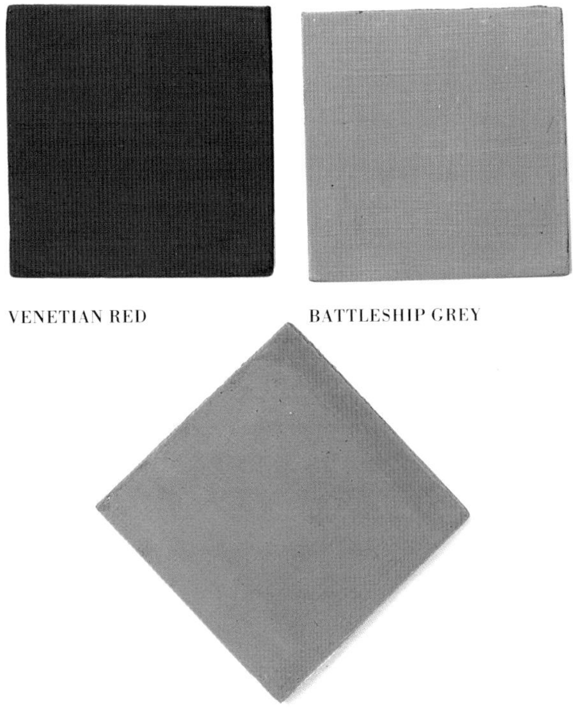

VENETIAN RED

BATTLESHIP GREY

GOLDEN YELLOW

Edwardian and Art Deco Colours

The colours of these two periods overlap, surprisingly
perhaps, with Edwardian colours persisting among old-
fashioned people till the late 1920s. The 'newest' colour of
this period is Signal Red, the first paint colour developed for
industrial use, and quite possibly the red enamel Mr Pooter
painted his bath with in *Diary of a Nobody* by George and
Weedon Grossmith. Blues and greens reappeared strongly in
the wake of Art Nouveau, as well as a clutch of strong
yellows, ranging from dainty Primrose to a lusty Golden
Yellow, which may have been influenced by Bakst's designs
for the Ballets Russes. For many people, however, Eau de Nil
combined with Deep Cream sum up the safe middlebrow
colourway which spread over walls of schools, hospitals and
other institutions and left an enduring period flavour that
lasted till after World War II. Art Deco 'fashionables' went
for tremendous contrasts of colour as well as endless
variations on a theme, such as a dozen shades of white, à la
Syrie Maugham, the fashionable decorator. Contrasts of
texture were popular and available, too, such as high gloss
with matt or eggshell. Glossy paints were indicated for
'hygiene', a new preoccupation of the time. A high-style Deco
room might have glossy black walls, Signal Red door with
Azure window treatments and geometric stencils.

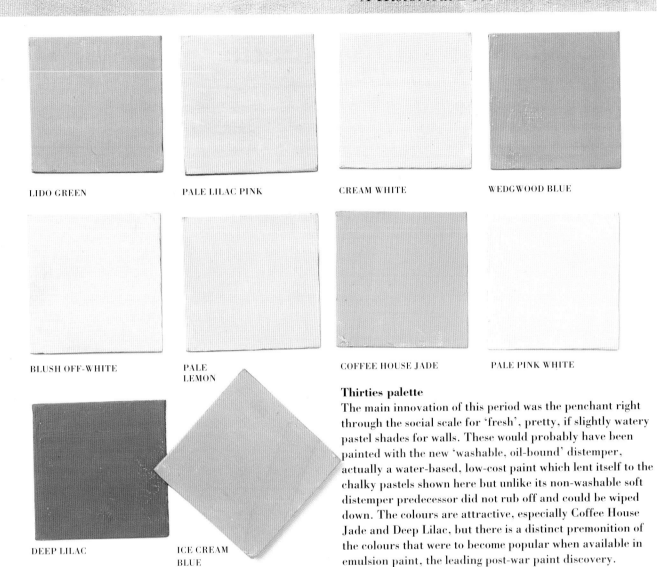

LIDO GREEN

PALE LILAC PINK

CREAM WHITE

WEDGWOOD BLUE

BLUSH OFF-WHITE

PALE LEMON

COFFEE HOUSE JADE

PALE PINK WHITE

DEEP LILAC

ICE CREAM BLUE

Thirties palette
The main innovation of this period was the penchant right through the social scale for 'fresh', pretty, if slightly watery pastel shades for walls. These would probably have been painted with the new 'washable, oil-bound' distemper, actually a water-based, low-cost paint which lent itself to the chalky pastels shown here but unlike its non-washable soft distemper predecessor did not rub off and could be wiped down. The colours are attractive, especially Coffee House Jade and Deep Lilac, but there is a distinct premonition of the colours that were to become popular when available in emulsion paint, the leading post-war paint discovery.

(*Continued from page 104.*) Anyone seriously interested in faithful, sensitive restoration of period decoration would be well advised to follow suit. Books, galleries, museums, historic buildings can all help sharpen one's eye and increase one's understanding of a particular epoch or, indeed, a particular place, because practices and usage may – and did – vary considerably from, say, Colonial America to Paris, Vienna or London at the same time. Such colours as Indian Red (a variant on the red oxide pigments used since ancient times) and Pumpkin Yellow remained fashionable and customary in America long after they had gone off the boil in Europe, which may well have been (since a bolder colour range remains an American preference to this day) an unconscious response to the very different quality of light on that side of the Atlantic.

Colour via the Media

ANYONE WHO USES, PLAYS OR DABBLES in paint media, either professionally or as a hobby, becomes aware that the same basic pigment, raw colour if you like, changes character and appearance and intensity to an extraordinary degree when used with different media. To demonstrate this, one good photograph is worth a thousand words, so we painted up a clutch of eggs, ordinary supermarket eggs, to show what we mean, graphically. Our idea was firstly to illustrate how media affect colour, and secondly to discover how much pigment is needed to tint paints of different composition. Also, I hope, the experiment gives some indication of how all these paints, old and new, look side-by-side, egg shaped. All the eggs were first primed with the same white acrylic primer, because white eggs are annoyingly unavailable in supermarkets, and we had to start with plain white for the variations to become clear. Over this we

The medium to which the blue pigment was added for the eleven eggs we painted is given next to each of them, with old and new media illustrated randomly alongside each other, for comparison.

MATT EMULSION

OIL SCUMBLE

ACRYLIC SCUMBLE

COPAL VARNISH

LIMEWASH

painted each egg with the same ultramarine powdered pigment, in the same measured quantity, dissolved in the same amount of whichever medium, as labelled in the photograph.

The widely varying results did justify the time. Visibly, blue pigment in a transparent oil medium delivers many times the colour intensity of the same amount of pigment in a chalky (distemper, gesso or casein/lime) base, and a little more than the same dose in an in-between base like scumble. Emulsion mixed and went on easily, but, interestingly, the final tint and texture look flat and heavy compared to those of the limewash.

The visual surprise in following our self-imposed discipline (same quantity of pigment relative to medium) was the disappearing act the pigment performed when added to media with a high chalk or white pigment base. Gesso and soft distemper emerged as nearly white. Pigment in varnish, especially high-gloss varnish, gave the most colour but were awkward to apply. Limewash/casein was interestingly textured but less appealing than limewash alone.

LIMEWASH/CASEIN

GESSO AND PIGMENT

EGG TEMPERA

TURPENTINE/LINSEED OIL/VARNISH

MATT POLYURETHANE VARNISH

SOFT DISTEMPER

Lead Paint

Although commercially produced lead-based oil paint is now on the forbidden list in the UK for all but owners of Grade I listed historic buildings, and fine artists like Lucian Freud who must have their flake white, it remains a paint of admirable and interesting qualities, used widely during the eighteenth century on all manner of surfaces, principally walls and woodwork. Visually, it has a distinctive quality, a soft, matt patina, increasing with age. As exterior paint, it developed a chalky bloom which, together with its gutsy texture, gave doors, window fames, shutters and so forth a quite special characteristic look. I suspect people struggle to re-create this effect, often without realizing what it is they are attempting to imitate.

Lead white is basic lead carbonate, one of the oldest artificial pigments, known to the Ancient Greeks. It was always an oil paint, indeed till the mid-nineteenth century (when zinc white was formulated) the only white oil-based pigment available to artists and

Plain and glossy as the white china cup and saucer your espresso comes in in an Italian café, this Mediterranean bathroom could not be more functional – shower cubicle, step-up bath. Yet despite the white, shiny finish everywhere it doesn't look the least bit clinical. Terracotta floor tiles help, but it's the generous gleaming white plastered and painted slab enclosing the bath that makes it look traditional and organic.

decorative painters. It has exceptional opacity, or covering power, mixes beautifully with pigments, has a heavy, clinging texture and is both durable and protective as a surfacing. Lead painted exteriors are still found in battered but reasonable condition dating from the early nineteenth century.

Lead paint in the eighteenth century was made by mixing white lead carbonate with linseed oil (raw, not boiled, as boiled darkens the colour immediately) and real turpentine. Coloured pigments, finely ground, were mixed with this white lead to give them body. Gritty pigments, like smalt made from powdered blue glass, combined more readily with lead white because of its 'buttery' texture.

Lead paint dried to a glossy sheen, but this rapidly dulled down in use. It had a

The restored paint scheme for the hallway to Pallant House, Chichester, was researched by the English paint historian Ian Bristow. The paints used were all lead-based, here tinted in subtly differing 'stone' or 'common colours'. The gloss derives from linseed oil in the paint formula, but will gradually lessen over time. A handsome Queen Anne town house, extensively and authentically restored, Pallant House should figure on the itinerary of anyone interested in seeing old houses painted in their original paints and colours.

tendency to yellow (due to the oil) especially where light could not reach it (under pictures, for instance). Often a little blue was added to counteract this. In the early eighteenth century lead paints were applied over both walls and woodwork (distemper being reserved for ceilings) but by the mid-eighteenth century it was chiefly used above dado level. The stony neutrals which remained first choice for halls and staircases were best done in lead white pigmented with ochres and lamp black, used in varying quantities.

There can be little doubt that we have lost a handsome, tough and characterful paint with the prohibition of lead in commercial manufacture. However, it is also well proven that lead was highly poisonous if its fumes were inhaled during the mixing, or if painters inadvertently swallowed the paint. People are more important than paint finishes. Two points, finally, need emphasizing. Stripping off early paint-work, which could well contain lead, should be done with a mask and gloves. And the nearest approximation to lead paint, visually, may well be a water-based emulsion paint, not too smoothly brushed out, treated to several coats of a matt acrylic varnish.

Oil Paint

Just when the use of paints made with oil as binder and spirits of turpentine as medium began to supersede other types, principally egg tempera, for fine art work is not known for certain. The sixteenth-century Italian art biographer Giorgio Vasari claimed that it was introduced by the Flemish school of painters, naming Jan van Eyck, but like most innovations it

A glossy paint finish at its most resplendent, sprayed, hand-rubbed and buffed to a mirror shine on a vintage Rolls Royce in deep blue picked out with white coachlines. Lining on body work as perfect as this was done by skilled painters who could paint fine lines freehand in one confident, practised movement. The old coach-painters made something of a minor art form, akin to calligraphy, of this refined type of decorative lining.

probably overlapped with older practices for some time, adopted by some painters more readily than others. Botticelli painted his delicious *Birth of Venus* in egg tempera, on a gessoed poplar panel; Titian, a few decades later, painted his sumptuous *Venus of Urbino* in oil on canvas.

Oil paints gave richer tones, with fine glazes achieving a new depth of modelling and realism, gorgeous flesh tones and finely rendered textures. Oil paint also permitted over-painting, adjustments, second thoughts, a new freedom. Artists, or their assistants, pre-pared paints and varnishes in the studio, grinding pigments to mix with various oils (poppy, walnut as well as linseed) and thinners like turpentine.

House paints bound with oil arrived later but were prepared in much the same way. It was early recognised that oil paints, especially those using lead white, were far more durable than the old distempers and limewashes, especially on wooden surfaces. Pigments were usually ground with oil in a mortar. More oil was added from time to time, and the paste when fine enough was transferred to a slab and ground still more finely with a stone, marble or glass muller. The mix was then worked through a linen cloth, or sieve. Some pigments could be ground more finely than others, which caused problems in colour

mixing. In general, old pigments were still ten times coarser than most modern pigments. The refractiveness, or brilliance, of many old paints is thought to relate to their large particle size.

Application was similarly painstaking. Turpentine was added to the oil/pigment paste to thin it enough to brush out, and to speed drying. As many as seven coats were applied, thinly, with 'fat' (more oil) alternating with 'lean', ending up with a fat coat using boiled linseed oil, which dried glossy but oxidized rapidly to a soft, matt finish.

A detail of painted cart wheels showing how coachlines could be used to emphasize and pick out interesting detail, and give a finished appearance to a complex piece of joinery. Gypsy caravans, canal boats and dog carts were usually treated to decorative lining as the finishing touch on their bright and natty paintwork.

Falun Red Shed

FALUN RÖTT, OR FALUN RED, is an excellent and unique traditional exterior paint for raw wood – unplaned timber straight from the saw – which has been used in Sweden for several hundred years, but until recently has scarcely been recognized, let alone employed, anywhere else in the world. The oversight is both surprising and regrettable, since Falun Red has everything to recommend it to owners of timber buildings, barns, sheds and garages, as well as wooden houses. It is relatively inexpensive: one coat onto raw timber is usually enough to cover and offers protection for seven to twelve years. It is non-toxic and environmentally friendly and it dries to a soft, matt red-brown colour of great warmth and dignity, which improves with age. Though the paint is water-based, it contains a high proportion, approximately eight per cent, of linseed oil, which helps to keep timber in good condition through Sweden's long, snowbound winter months. Almost every wooden cottage in rural Sweden is finished with this paint today, and its rich, robin red-breast colouring is extraordinarily effective, visually, on clusters of little houses and barns in their forest setting, equally vivid against winter snow or the translucent greens of a Scandinavian spring. This must be the original of the much-loved Barn Red that strikes a warm traditional note along America's Eastern seaboard.

The source of Falun Rött is the Kopparberget mine in Sweden's central Dalarna. Kopparberget literally means 'copper mountain', and the ore has been mined there for centuries. The paint is a spin-off from the mining process: waste from the mine, discarded because of its low copper content, has weathered over centuries to produce a red earth pigment containing red ochre (iron oxide) together with silicic acid, whose presence adds to the stability and richness of its colouring. Washed, roasted and refined, the mineral pigment gives the paint its unique coloration, so typically Swedish that the celebrated playwright, August Strindberg, quite seriously proposed that the Swedish flag should be Falun red and green, a suggestion which clearly fell on deaf ears, since the national colours are blue and yellow.

Like many good inventions, Falun Rött began life as a luxury commodity, a status symbol used on Swedish wooden palaces and great houses in the seventeenth century, in a touching attempt to mimic the ruddy fashionable colouring of northern European bricks. It was not until the nineteenth century that this admired finish became available to the bourgeoisie and peasantry, and the previously weathered wood colouring of boarded cottages and farms, neutral as wild bird feathers, took on this characteristic 'ruddle' colouring. To begin with, making up the paint from the powder pigment was a highly regional affair, its components varying from village to village. Ingredients have the characteristic alchemical oddity – seaweed, urine, vitriol – which are doubtless proven over time since some are retained in the modern product. Though the red colouring has prevailed, the

This quaint structure – shed, kiosk or bothy depending on your point of view – stands outside the window, opposite my desk. Made of rough sawn timber, previously treated to a patchy coat of wood preservative, it became the guinea-pig for a trial run of Falun Rött. We added the china-blue trellis – not typically Swedish – to emphasize its faintly chinoiserie appearance. Bowered in greenery, including a weeping birch and several potted plants, it gives my tiny slice of urban garden a nostalgic reminder of Scandinavian journeys. The paint went on like a dream and dried in twenty minutes, leaving a pleasant whiff of linseed oil.

Falun range now includes variants – Falun Light, Falun Ochre and Falun Terra, with the same properties as their excellent predecessor.

In my view this is a paint of so many practical as well as aesthetic virtues, being cheap and easy to apply, as well as highly protective even in the fiercest Nordic winters, that it deserves to be recognized more widely throughout all countries belonging to what is known as the 'conifer culture', especially perhaps in the northern states of the USA, and in Canada.

Colouring Limewash

THE MOST SATISFYING COLOURS in limewash are the simple, old earth and mineral colours shown in the 'Fresco' palette on page 105. Used alone, or intermixed, these give the warm, unforced shades that have been used for centuries inside and out. In vivid sunlight, a sharper pastel shade – turquoise, washed-out blues, greens, flowery pinks – seems more appropriate, while warmer colours – earthy ochres, terracottas, orange, warm pinks – have a comforting glow under greyer skies. Mixing is simple if you go slowly with the tinting, testing results on paper dried over heat. Limewash always dries paler. Also, three or more coats are needed to build colour intensity. If wash colour varies slightly from coat to coat, this adds to the charm. There is no need to match previous coats exactly, but stay within harmonizing shades.

You will need

■ Powder pigments
Pots or jars for
dissolving pigments in
water ■ Spoon, whisk
■ Bucket for mixing
■ Gloves, goggles
■ Paper for testing

3 *A larger quantity of the same dissolved pigments can then be added to the limewash. Begin by adding the pigments gradually, slowly building up the colour. If the pigments have not been thoroughly dissolved this will distort the final colour.*

1 *The raw ingredients for making limewash include mature putty lime, well beaten up to disperse lumps and give a smooth texture. To this enough water is added to bring the mix to a milky consistency, and well stirred; thin coats are better than thick. Other ingredients include powder pigments. We blended yellow ochre with a little raw sienna and marigold (a deep orange) for this soft yellow limewash.*

2 *The pigments are thoroughly dissolved in water. To determine the right proportions add gradually to a test sample of limewash then test on a piece of paper. Earth pigments dissolve readily in water.*

4 *The limewash is then whisked thoroughly. The tinted limewash with fresco pigments can be stored indefinitely without any effect. Some blues, however, may change colour slightly over time and should be used all at once. Once on the wall, the colour is stable. Dampen all walls before painting. Use a large fibre brush and slap it on in all directions.*

Limewashed walls have an extraordinary quality, managing to look soft, rich, but ethereal all at once. Applied correctly – thin coats on damp walls – the finish is not powdery, but solid.

Making Soft Distemper

A S THE PUBLIC INTEREST in 'green' paint grows (and there are signs that it is taking off both in Europe and the USA already) my prediction is that this simple, pretty and wholly natural old-fashioned paint will come leaping back into favour. It is very easy to make, as our pictures here show; the materials are widely available and its soft 'brushy' texture is ideally suited to the countrified look that people like today. Pastel shades make up beautifully in a soft distemper; for stronger colours use the colour-washing technique. Stencilling works well on distempered walls. You can use acrylic colours to stencil with, or make your own from powder pigments and the same distemper base.

You will need

■ Whiting ■ Rabbit skin glue granules ■ Pigments ■ Double boiler ■ Heatproof bowls ■ Hand whisk or electric whisk or power tool

1 *Whiting is poured into a container – use a bucket or extra-large bowl to make large quantities – half-filled with water, stopping when the powder 'peaks' above the surface. Leave to soak and absorb wateer overnight.*

2 *At the same time pour water over rabbit skin glue granules to cover, and leave overnight to fatten. They will swell up to many times their original bulk.*

3 *The soaked rabbit skin glue is put to melt over low heat in an improvised double boiler, here a bowl set over a pan of simmering water. Stir from time to time with a wooden spoon.*

4 *This shows the glue size completely dissolved, and looking rather like thick honey. Put the melted size through a coarse sieve to remove any undissolved lumps.*

5 *Any unabsorbed water on top of the whiting is poured off, and the soaked whiting thoroughly stirred for several minutes. For large quantities use a propellor attachment on a variable-speed power drill for mixing.*

6 *The next step is to combine the melted size with the whiting. It is important that the size is left to cool down for twenty minutes or so before mixing, otherwise there is a risk of the size gelling again when it makes contact with the cold whiting.*

7 *Dry pigments used for tinting, and shown in the previous picture unmixed, are soaked in water, then thoroughly blended – an old electric blender could come in useful – and added to the distemper mix.*

The peaceful charm of a small London study owes a lot to the velvety texture and aquamarine tint of a home-made soft distemper. Powder pigments in ultramarine, yellow and raw sienna were used for tinting the paint. The painted floor, using standard emulsion (latex) paint, was coloured to harmonize with the walls and reflect light back into the north-facing space.

8 *Use a large standard brush to apply distemper. A soft brush gives a smoother finish, while a traditional fibre brush gives a more textured effect. As this detail shows, distemper has excellent covering power. Dry colour samples beforehand because wet distemper is almost twice as dark as dry.*

Impasto Paint

You will need

■ Impasto Paint
■ 'Ochre' and 'New
Apricot' Paint Magic
Colourwashes ■ Sponge
and softening brush
■ Fine grade wet-and-
dry abrasive paper

I MPASTO IS THE technical word used to describe a thickly-textured build-up of paint on a canvas. Some painters work almost wholly in impasto, like Van Gogh; Rembrandt, on the other hand, brushed on isolated thick squiggles of paint as a highlight on a lace ruff or nightcap. Impasto is sensuous, paint (usually oil) heavy, the brushwork a map of artistic intent.

What we are talking about here is a little different. My paint company dreamed up a gently textured base paint for our Colourwash a while back, with watery Mediterranean finishes over rough plaster in mind. We named it Impasto. I love it, and use it in my own home constantly. When I saw how antique dealer and restorer Freya Robins of Swaffer Antiques had decorated rooms in her own house in Arundel, Sussex, with this formula, we sent a photographer to record them. It seemed only fair, in a book so preoccupied with the real, right, tradition-al way to get a particular effect, that we should give space to a quick, easy, state-of-the-art paint job that looks almost as good. Impasto as base, roughed up a little, colourwashed, then rubbed back just a touch so that some base shows through is the most appealing, up-dated version available.

1 *Over a dry base coat of Impasto, brushed on as standard paint but more thickly, a vivid yellow Colourwash (mixed from Ochre and Apricot) is washed over loosely with a decorator's sponge.*

2 *A softening brush is used to blend, smooth and even up the still wet Colourwash – not too much, but enough for an even colour overall. The Impasto texture helps.*

3 *A detail shows how the vivid but kindly colour settles down in context, rubbed back with sandpaper when dry so just spots and tags of the off-white Impasto base show through.*

Freya is sold on this paint effect, and the vivid charm of her home gives me the unsolicited approval I need to describe the process here. I like the way she uses it and hope that you do too.

Another view of the Impasto/Colourwash treatment, making
an appealing backdrop to the Swaffer collection of eclectic,
desirable, mostly French furniture, bric-à-brac and
'kitchenalia'. A Van Gogh/Monet yellow wall colour seems to
pull it all together.

Painting and Distressing

You will need

■ Shellac ■ Off-white water-based basecoat ■ Wax candle ■ Wire wool ■ Grey-green water-based paint ■ Terracotta water-based paint ■ Selection of brushes ■ Egg Tempera ■ Red, blue, yellow and raw umber paint pigments ■ Acrylic matt varnish ■ Antiquing wax

D ISTRESSED, A TERM ONCE applied to gentlewomen, now more often denotes paintwork which has been deliberately abraded or cracked to suggest the battered looks of a surface attacked by time, use and sunlight. Anathemized by the old school of painters trained to apply a flawless surface, distressing, on furniture especially, is very popular with a public which responds to the colourfulness of painted pieces yet prefers them to look worn, weathered and ancestral. Visually, distressed paint layers present a satisfying complexity, and items treated in this way settle effortlessly into a room without that jarring note of brand newness. Distressing techniques are popular with furniture makers, too, because they can be used to disguise the fact that low-cost furniture is largely made up of reconstituted boards, melamine, MDF, etc. Straightforward paint also does this, but lacks mellowness.

1 *Our corner cupboard is a typical reproduction piece – part ply, part veneer, part MDF. Stained and French polished, it looks tacky. Distressing with water-based paints takes not much longer and confers a rustic dignity. We substituted glass shelves for the shaped MDF ones.*

2 *We chose a gentle, Scandinavian colour scheme. A base coat of off-white was brushed directly over bare wood, though all the MDF was first sealed with shellac.*

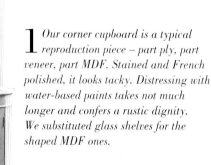

3 *The base coat piece, when dry, is rubbed all over with an ordinary household candle. The wax acts as a parting agent between the base coat and the top coat, which gives a fashionable two-tone look when rubbed back. Rub wax on liberally, so it shows, thickest on mouldings and leading edges where wear would occur.*

6 Pads of medium fine wire wool rubbed firmly over the dry grey-green remove any paint applied over the wax parting agent in an easy but natural-looking way. This should be continued over the entire piece.

4 *The grey-green top coat is brushed on top of the waxed base coat thickly enough to cover it completely. We used a smaller angled brush to get into mouldings on cornice and glazing bars. The oval door panel was left bare to this point but is now filled in with off-white.*

5 *For warmth and contrast, and as a background to china or glass, the base-coated top cabinet is treated differently. A water-based glaze in terra-cotta is applied over the off-white, and softened with a softening brush to disperse streaks and blotches.*

7 *Apples seem suitably countrified as decoration. A black-and-white image was enlarged on the photocopier to fit the oval cartouche, then traced onto tracing paper. We scribbled on the back with soft lead pencil then laid the image on face-up and re-drew with a sharp pencil, leaving a faint but clear outline.*

MAKING EGG TEMPERA

Egg tempera is an ancient, simple and satisfying paint, combining the transparency and non-yellowing properties of pure watercolour with something of the unctuousness and smoothness of oils. Once fully dried, it is one of the toughest of all media. It is highly recommended for decorative work as being less plastic-looking than acrylic. With practice, making it becomes routine.

1 *Crack an egg, separating white and yolk carefully without breaking the membrane round the yolk. Roll the yolk in your palms gently, to dry off the albumen.*

2 *Pick up the yolk sac over a clean bowl and pinch to release the runny yolk. Add clean water, approximately twice the volume of yolk, and mix well.*

3 *Colours are made by mixing dry pigments with the eggy binder in separate containers. Use pigment cautiously and test on paper.*

8 *More flowing than acrylic colour, tougher than gouache in gum arabic (this requires spray fixative to seal), egg tempera shares their watercolour transparency, making it a good choice for applied decoration over pale backgrounds. Used thinly, as here, it dries rapidly with a matt finish. We chose colours that echo the cupboard paints – sludgy greens, pale orange-red with raw umber shadowing to paint the apples. Use good-quality, soft but springy watercolour brushes for tempera painting, with a fine one for detail. Decoration of this sort should not dominate; stand back from time to time to gauge the balance. It is helpful to take a break before applying the final touches: seeing the work afresh often points up where it needs strengthening or adjustment.*

9 *The outline of the cartouche needs emphasizing so the tempera mixture, tinted brownish-black, is used for lining freehand with a small lining brush. This has longer hairs than the standard watercolour brush, and holds more paint, allowing a line to continue further unbroken. It would be easier to work on a horizontal surface, unscrewing the door and laying it flat on a table.*

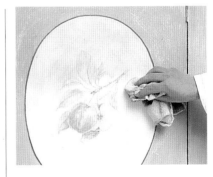

10 *A watery wash of green, with a little raw umber is applied over the oval cartouche then the cupboard is given a coat of matt acrylic varnish and a rub-over with dark antiquing wax.*

The finished cupboard, packed with china and glass, looks at home in a painted setting. The harlequin design on the walls was marked out with narrow masking tape, then colour-washed in colours including the green and terracotta of the cupboard itself. Using transparent colour like this ensures that the colours complement each other and are not too instrusive.

Woodgraining and Marbling

You will need

WOODGRAINING
■ Shrimp pink eggshell basecoat ■ Oil scumble glaze ■ White spirit ■ Burnt umber, Kassell earth, Mars black, carmine lake artist's oil colours ■ nylon brush and badger hair softener
MARBLING ■ Off-white eggshell basecoat ■ Paynes gray, ivory black & titanium white artist's oil colours ■ Oil-based scumble glaze ■ White spirit ■ Ivory black Conte crayon ■ Badger hair softener ■ Hog's-hair artist's brush ■ Long-haired sable brush ■ Decorator's brush ■ Clear polyurethane varnish

O F ALL THE FACTITIOUS USES of decorative paint, or *faux* finishes, the most demanding of technical skill are those of that élite branch of decorative painters known as 'marblers and grainers'. Usually, though not invariably, the two specialized skills went together, the same man being employed to treat columns and dado to a sienna or *vert antique* finish as to paint, glaze and soften doors of pine or deal to simulate a more precious wood, like mahogany. Most painterly marbling is generally Italian. They are familiar with different stones and their sense of scale and drama give their work a bold facility which 'reads' like marble at a distance, without being fussily literal. But the best grainers have often been British or Scandinavian, from timber rather than marble cultures. We combined both skills on one piece, a pine kitchen cabinet.

1 *After one coat of oil-based undercoat, filled and rubbed back, two coats of shrimp-pink eggshell, also sanded, made a smooth base for a rich dark mahogany graining.*

2 *A brown transparent glaze, made from oil scumble thinned with approximately 20% white spirit and tinted with burnt umber and Kassell earth is brushed over with a nylon brush.*

3 *From a palette including Mars black, carmine lake and the other colours, 'striping' begins, picking up a little more of this or that tint each time, but not obtrusively. Striping is done first from left to right, then right to left, for variety and naturalness.*

4 *Here the vital 'softening' is shown, using a badger softener worked across and along the stripes to blend and create 'ripples'. Two or three coats of polyurethane varnish are applied at the end for protection.*

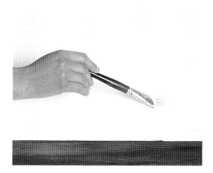

Marbling

1 *Over an off-white eggshell base, a slightly fantasized Carrara is in progress (bluish-grey on a yellowish base, I call it Gorgonzola). Here, using a hog's-hair artist's brush, the veining, using Paynes gray, ivory black and titanium white in a mix of 60% scumble, 40% white spirit, is streaked across the still wet eggshell base.*

2 *The veining proceeds rapidly in a loose, asymmetrical, naturalistic style across the top, using all colours on the brush at once, and alternately, for emphasis and variety. Don't overwork – keep referring to real marble.*

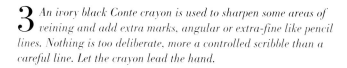

3 *An ivory black Conte crayon is used to sharpen some areas of veining and add extra marks, angular or extra-fine like pencil lines. Nothing is too deliberate, more a controlled scribble than a careful line. Let the crayon lead the hand.*

4 *The softener is played across and with the veining, firmly but gently, to open out shapes, make dark lines muzzier and introduce a happenstance element. This is the critical moment: too much loses dynamism, too little looks unconvincing. Finish with two or three coats of clear polyurethane.*

5 *The marbling has already begun to adopt an authentic feel. But to add the 'cold' quality of real marble to the work, using the small artist's brush apply a few selectively placed blobs of weakly diluted titanium white across the existing bluish-grey veins*

6 *With the hog's-hair artist's brush begin to add a few selectively placed 'streaks' of titanium white. These should be applied more heavily than the 'veins', using a bolder, looser stroke but keep a check on the work by stepping away occasionally for the overall picture.*

Here our cupboard sits in a traditionally 'rustic' setting, a solid workmanlike piece that fits comfortably into a French-style farmhouse kitchen. It demonstrates the adaptability of the skills of both marbling and graining traditionally used to mimic more sophisticated finishes for rather grand purposes. Our cupboard has pulled together both skills to create an unpretentious item of furniture.

8 *Once again use the badger softener to pull the work together by gently brushing out any harsh lines. The finished effect should convey the gentle but striking quality that marble possesses. Two or three coats of clear polyurethane varnish (yellowing is not a problem here) gives final protection.*

7 *Now again take the hog's-hair brush to begin to loosen and work out the blobs of white. Gently work the paint into streaks, allowing them to not only run with the direction of the veins but to occasionally cut across them, adding a feeling of depth to the overall effect.*

A Grecian Mural

ONTEMPORARY MURAL painters frequently use projected photographic slides of architectural subjects to help with painting perspective and shadowing. It struck me that the same trick would work brilliantly for a purely linear image, and classical Greek red-figure ceramic painting leapt to mind. There is a certain excitement in enlarging an image not much bigger than a playing card to an almost lifesize mural.

You will need

■ Colour slide images
■ Slide projector
■ Water-based paints and glazes ■ Acrylic colours ■ Flow Extender
■ Sable brushes

1 *Alternative images are laid out for inspection and the final choice – which I christen Senator and Faun – about to be photographed with slide film. This was done under studio lights, but a close-up under good natural light would also be fine.*

3 *A water-based glaze in terracotta is brushed on and softened for reasonably even texture over the Greek figures. Then the outlines are worked over with fine sable brushes and black acrylic, with Flow Extender added to make the brushstrokes finer and more fluent.*

2 *The projected image is distinct enough to draw around with a soft pencil on the pale wall surface. The next step is to wash over the background with diluted acrylic colour to firm up and clarify the drawing.*

4 *Finally, the background is gone over with an opaque black water-based paint with some burnt umber added to soften the contrast and give a more natural ceramic tint.*

The vision of an unknown Greek ceramic painter is translated into a mural decoration any patient copyist can achieve.

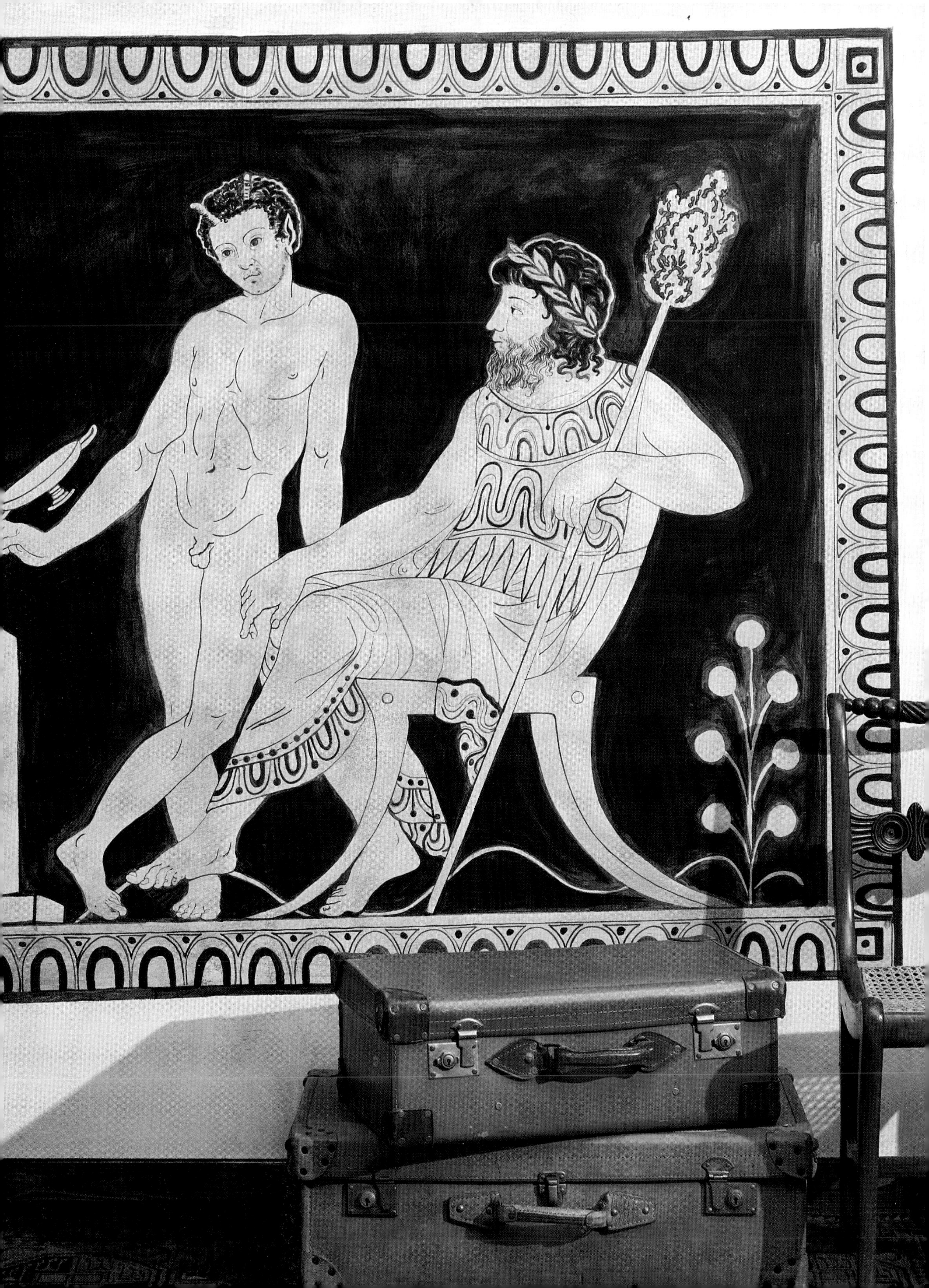

Finishing

TRADITIONALLY TRAINED PAINTERS ARE eloquent about the need to prepare a surface for painting with exemplary thoroughness, filling, priming, sanding, and so on. That a paint finish is only as good as its groundwork is a favourite pronouncement, with which I would not disagree. It is heart-rending to lavish time and effort on a superlative painted finish, like japanning, only to have the laboriously achieved, deeply glossy colour crack or blister off in use simply because one ignored this traditional wisdom.

The finishing tricks or techniques which formed part of the skilled traditional painter's repertoire are too valuable and interesting to be laid aside in the rush to transform dowdy kitchen units overnight. It matters that we understand and respect the patient craftsmanship and self-discipline that underwrote the magnificent examples of antique decorative painting, japanning and gilding. My object is not so much to conscript a new generation of skilled craftsmen as to show people intent on mimicking the real thing with cheaper materials and tricks of the trade just what it is they are counterfeiting and where they should pull the stops out and where employ a helpful, murky 'antiquing' stratagem. This is by no means a counsel of despair. An artfully faked-up (Dutch Metal over red paint) version of authentic water gilding (gold leaf over red clay) can be made to look more like a genuine antique – dirty, worn, aged – than newly applied gold leaf over gesso, with its high-voltage gleam.

THE SUBSTANCES DISCUSSED HERE are just some of the fine artist's traditional 'pharmacopoeia', mainly natural products developed over centuries for use in every stage of painting. They range from primer to varnish, for easing technical problems such as drying time or yellowing. Even today, when 'convenience' paints, like convenience food, have made so many laborious old procedures unnecessary, there will always be painters drawn to experiment with time-tested materials and recipes.

Oils, Gums, Resins and Glues

Nowadays many painters work in acrylic media, for good, practical reasons. These dry fast and solidly and are versatile enough to be used with gels for impasto effects, with retardants to slow drying time, and with 'flow enhancers' to add fluency, the outstanding property of oil paint. But while paint chemists maintain that acrylics are outstandingly durable, and light-fast, the whole technology is still new enough for their case to be unproven.

Fine art methods and materials have always tended to filter down to decorative painters, and even to house painters. The use of glazes is a classic instance. Titian used thirty to forty glazes on a painting; the marbler and grainer might use two or three; while the decorative effects painter gets his distressed wall finishes with one.

Oils

Linseed oil, expressed from flax seeds, comes in various grades: raw, boiled, or refined. This is the toughest and generally most satisfactory binding oil for making paint adhere. Turpentine – nowadays white spirit – is added to make the paint flow and dry to a flat film. Refined linseed oil is the least yellowing, and purest, and used mainly by artists. Boiled linseed oil, mainly used by house painters, differs in that it has driers added. Other oils used by artists and paint manufacturers include walnut and poppy seed.

Gums

Hardened sap or exudation from various trees and shrubs, gums differ from resins in being water-soluble but insoluble in volatile solvents like alcohol, turpentine and white spirit. Gum arabic and gum tragacanth are used as binders for watercolours like gouache and as adhesives, sizes and stiffeners. Gum arabic, like clearcole (see page 159), dries to a glossy finish, makes a clear, pretty, fast-drying transparent vehicle for decorative work (flowers, etc) but needs sealing with shellac and varnish. Gum tragacanth is largely an industrial additive.

Resins

Natural resins, which include the endlessly useful shellac, as well as copal, damar and rosin, are soluble, unlike gums, in alcohol, turpentine, etc, but insoluble in water. They are widely used in commercial varnishes. Shellac, obtainable in flake as well as liquid form, dissolves in methylated spirits (denatured alcohol), is a fast-drying (20 minutes) shiny but brittle coating varnish, much used as an isolating varnish in decorative paint systems and as the main ingredient in French polishing.

The materials and equipment shown here were used on our japanned box. These include gesso for priming, acrylic paints for colouring, two types of shellac (Button Polish and White Polish) soft brushes, methylated spirits (denatured alcohol) for diluting shellac, wet-and-dry paper, finest wire wool and powdered rottenstone for final burnishing and smoothing.

RED ACRYLIC PAINT

BLUE ACRYLIC PAINT

BUTTON POLISH

SOFT CLOTH

WIRE WOOL

METHYLATED SPIRITS

WET-AND-DRY PAPER

ROTTEN STONE

WHITE POLISH/SHELLAC

GESSO

SOFT BRUSHES

A selection of oils, gums, resins and glues

OIL OF LAVENDER

DRYING POPPY OIL

ESSENCE OF TURPENTINE

BOILED LINSEED OIL

REFINED LINSEED OIL

SEEDLAC

DRAGONS BLOOD

LEMON SHELLAC

GUM ARABIC

RABBIT SKIN GLUE

LACTIC CASEIN

PEARL GLUE

ROSIN

Glues

Casein, a milk by-product, is an extremely tenacious binder or adhesive, used as a glue in the joinery trade. As a paint binder, combined with pigments, it gives a crude but gutsy matt paint with great covering power: the original 'buttermilk' paint. Casein, in the form of skim milk, is added to limewash in small quantities to increase weather resistance. Rabbit-skin glue is usually sold in granules. A traditional ingredient of gesso, it is a powerful adhesive for sticking fabrics paper, etc, as well as more traditional materials. Pearl Glue is an animal size, less refined than rabbit-skin glue, consisting of attractive-looking amber coloured granules, which need to be soaked in water and then melted in a double boiler for use. Cheaper than rabbit-skin glue, it adds an amber tint, which could interfere with the final colouring.

Lacquer and Japanning

ALTHOUGH THE WORD LACQUER tends to bring to mind decorative articles of beauty rather than utility, the earliest recorded use of this curious oriental tree sap was entirely functional. It was used to coat baskets, filling in the weave to transport food in ancient China. The sap is taken from various species of the Rhus tree, relatives of the Sumach. The raw sap is greyish and toxic, causing dermatitis if handled incautiously. After straining, it is stored in air-tight containers and matured, sometimes for years. Over time the colour darkens to a brownish-black. Thick and sticky in its raw state, the sap applied to a surface and left to cure in the necessary dark and damp conditions develops exceptional hardness, perhaps the unique characteristic of oriental lacquer. Hardness increases with the number and depth of applications. Thirty to forty layers might result, with rubbing down, in a final coating, over a light wooden core, only two

Right: 'Lacquered' walls in decorator's parlance mean walls painted and glazed for a rich depth of colour, followed by many coats of gloss varnish, rubbed back scrupulously until a highly reflective, shiny, smooth finish is achieved. The walls must also be perfect to start with, smoothly plastered and free of cracks, dents and lumps. It is a sophisticated look, usually chosen for dining rooms where shiny walls and twinkling candlelight make a dramatic setting for formal meals.

Left: This magnificent eight-panelled lacquer screen is by the designer Eileen Gray, one of a handful of Europeans to have learnt the art of lacquering in the authentic oriental way. She studied for several years with Sugawara, a young Japanese lacquerist whom she met in Paris in 1906. Black lacquer with gold and silver decoration is a highly traditional combination but Eileen Gray has given it her own modern, even Cubist, interpretation here.

millimetres in thickness. For the carved lacquer which the Chinese most admired, a little cheating was indulged – vegetable ash was mixed in with lacquer base coats as a quicker way to build up a thick surface for carving.

Only five pigments are suitable chemically for tinting lacquer – red, green, yellow, gold and brown. Black, perhaps to Western eyes the most typical lacquer colour, is created by the natural darkening of the matured sap. Fourteenth- and fifteenth-century Chinese lacquerwork was usually made in different coloured layers, so that carving down through the material created contrasts that threw the work into more dramatic relief, such as black incised decoration against a red ground.

True oriental lacquer began arriving in Europe in the sixteenth and seventeenth centuries, soon becoming a profitable import trade. Europeans already had painted, carved and inlaid furniture, but nothing quite like these oriental wares – screens, panels, boxes – with their exquisite workmanship, fantastic decoration and flawlessly glossy surfaces. The hard, perfect surface must always have remained the real desideratum, but in the wake of a fashionable appetite for these exotic artefacts, European tradesmen, cabinetmakers, joiners, painters and gilders quite rapidly evolved a type of decorated furniture which superficially resembled its prototypes and came to be known as 'japan'. The style of decoration, confusingly, was Chinese, and recognised as such under the generic term 'chinoiserie', but the glossy surface treatment, which gave the illusion of impeccable lacquer, was christened 'japanning'.

The most widely used varnish in japanning was shellac, which was fast-drying, highly glossy and transparent. A japanned piece, with raised, gilded or coloured decoration in the chinoiserie manner – islets linked by fretwork bridges, where tiny figures in pointed hats carrying parasols strolled under drooping willows – would be given maybe twenty to thirty shellac varnishings, rubbed back and smoothed until they gleamed enticingly. But shellac is brittle, stained by water and alcohol; the most painstaking japanning could never begin to emulate the jet hardness and imperviousness of oriental lacquer. However, it was pretty, colourful and charming, and japanned European pieces found ready buyers. Japanners were quick to exploit the special possibilities of their technique, using a much wider colour range, such as deep peacock blue, vivid yellow, scarlet and vermilion. Decoration ran riot, too. Few later designers have attempted work in genuine lacquer, for

Below: Equipment used for contemporary oriental lacquering is shown on the left. The top tray holds glass phials with metal powder, flakes and dry tinting colours. Below, tools include mixing spatulas, and iron needle engravers, a set of mounted teeth – rat, Thai fish and wolf – for burnishing and incising, grey stone for polishing and smoothing raised decoration. The top right tray holds samples of tinted raw lacquer, a quire of specialist brushes and bamboo sieves for blowing metal powder onto the work.

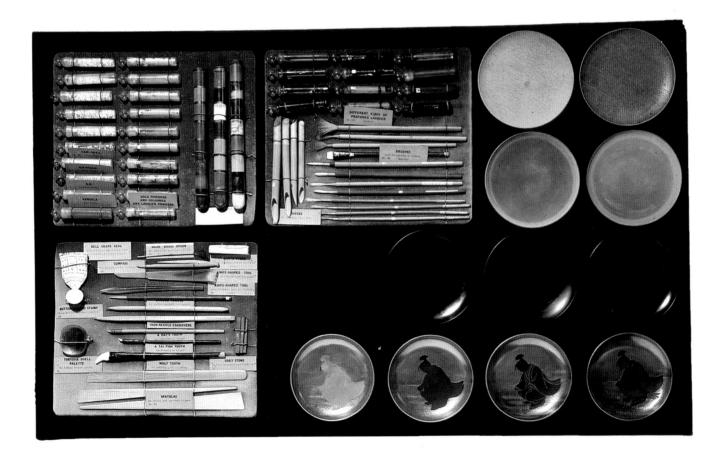

obvious reasons. The dedicated and brilliant English designer Eileen Gray suffered painful dermatitis as a result of her determination to learn and execute the craft. Her lacquered screens, couches and tables are now museum pieces, noble proof that the most ancient materials and techniques can be re-invented in the proper spirit, creatively, with innovative and dazzling results.

Pastiglia

PASTIGLIA IS AN ITALIAN TERM, literally meaning 'pasty, doughlike', used to denote raised decoration in low-relief executed in gesso on a gessoed ground. Enrichment of this sort was used on many of the religious paintings of the early Renaissance, usually on details such as haloes and jewels, to be finished in gold-leaf or tempera. Italian painters had discovered that gold-leaf on raised, tooled or punched surfaces reflected the light of altar candles much more scintillatingly than leaf laid on flat. A gesso foundation had just enough resilience to be impressed with special little decorative punches without breaking or tearing the fragile gold-leaf. The process is described in a treatise of 1437 by Cennino Cennini.

Building up shapes with gesso is patient work, however, entailing not one continuous application but lots of brief attentions over a longish time span. The first brushwork fills in the drawn shape, subsequent touches worked gradually towards the centre, to create a rounded shape not more than a few millimetres high, or 'proud'. The gesso layers need to dry out to the proper 'thirsty' stage each time (nearly, but not quite, dry). This process

Below: Starting at the top right of the opposite page and progressing across and down line by line are the thirty-five stages involved in making a gilded and coloured lacquer sake cup with raised decoration. As the picture shows, sixteen separate stages are needed in the way of priming and filling before the first full coat of black lacquer goes on and a further nineteen before the piece is complete. Lacquer is still being made today, in Japan especially – but not surprisingly high-quality pieces are very expensive.

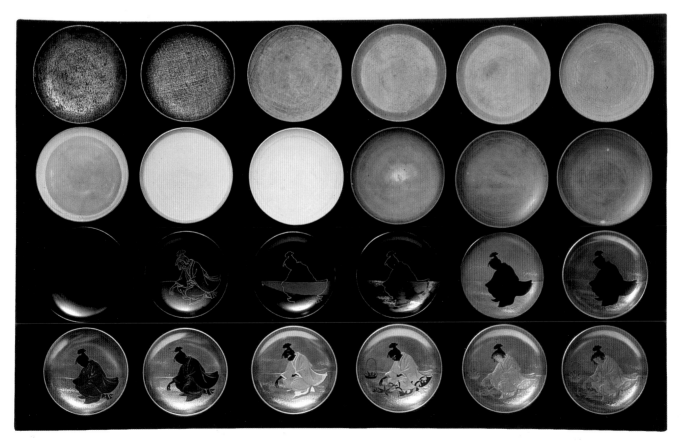

needs careful judging because drying time varies with the season and the weather, and the final pastiglia shapes need whittling and scraping and smoothing with small metal tools to clear off roughness and define the shapes more clearly. All this before laying on an appropriate bole and the metal leaf itself.

Today, pastiglia as Duccio, Botticelli or Cennini knew it is almost as remote as alchemy. Even the less exacting techniques of the eighteenth century would be too labour-intensive and expensive for all but the grandest work for the richest clients. Recent technical advances have thrown up short cuts, using fast-drying, hard-setting compounds, with an acrylic content, that can with a little adjustment and experiment give a comparable effect in a fraction of the time. Acrylic modelling compounds, obtainable from any good artist's suppliers, stick firmly, dry hard and can be brushed on like gesso, layer after layer, with good results. The disadvantage is that they dry so hard that much more forceful final shaping is needed, using files, blades and sandpaper, than with the more powdery and yielding gesso of the old pastiglia. And they look harder, too, with a gritty surface that is not suitable for gold-leaf. One solution here is to coat the pastiglia shapes with a final layer of gesso, to refine the texture, or even a coat of household fine surface filler, always applied with a brush.

The speeding-up approach continues through the current practice of finishing the pastiglia. A tough, acrylic, water-based paint will often be used instead of the bole, in a similar colour; a fast-acting size may be used to fasten the leaf – often Dutch Metal or even gold paint – rather than the old, temperamental size which has to be watched for the right degree of 'tack'. Some painters use Rotring pens to draw on the detail, using a blast of

Regular Gold Leaf (reading form top left clockwise this shows)-
1 Burnished
2 Burnished and distressed
3 Matt and distressed
4 Matt

fixative to stabilise it before final varnishing. However, when aiming for a japanned look, it is still usual to finish a piece off with several coats of shellac, much the same as the old japanners used, because this dries almost as quickly as any acrylic or polyurethane varnish and adds a mellow tint to the work. It is a finish that responds to careful rubbing down. This dulls shellac glitziness, cleans off grit and dust, and gives a warm, subdued lustre that matches the look of antique 'japan'. There must be some loss of quality and character when a complex process is shortened so drastically, but at first glance a cleverly produced imitation of eighteenth-century japan is by no means unworthy. What is still open to question is whether it will age as gracefully.

Metallic Finishes

OF ALL THE PRECIOUS METALS, gold has always, historically, been the most prized; not only for its market value, as the chosen currency and symbol of wealth and power, but also, surely, for its beauty, especially when the metal was soft, pure, and worked exquisitely,

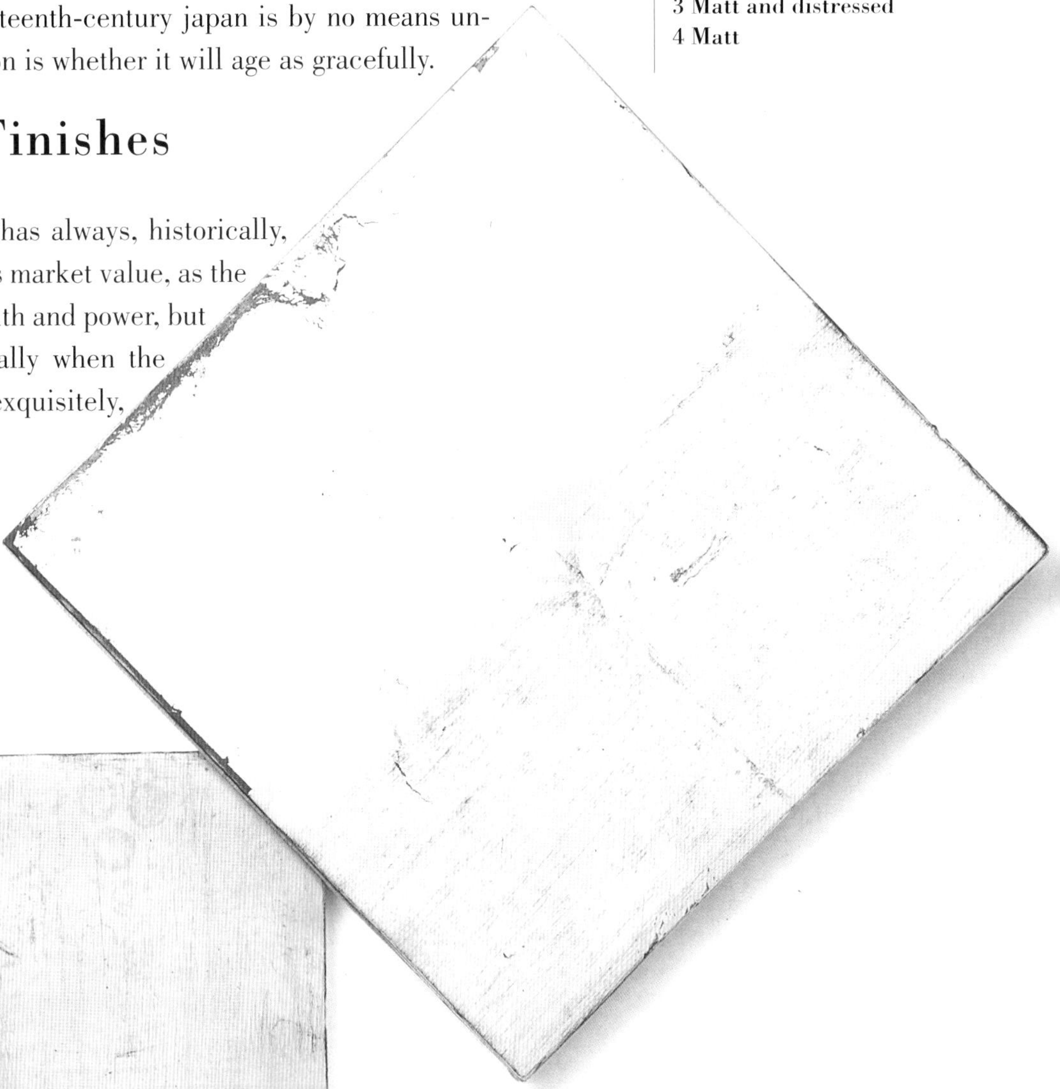

Red Gold (Rouge)
(From top left clockwise)
1 Burnished
2 Burnished and distressed
3 Matt and distressed
4 Matt

Lemon Gold
(From top left clockwise)
1 Burnished
2 Burnished and distressed
3 Matt and distressed
4 Matt

as it is in so much ancient jewellery and ornament. The radiance of gold, as the ancients used it, before ways of adulterating it with alloys were arrived at, is truly spectacular. Examples can be seen in museums everywhere; one of the most memorable is a diadem, or wreath, of myrtle leaves and flowers excavated at Vergina, in Macedonia and exhibited in the Archaeological Museum of Thessalonica. Vergina was the royal capital of Philip, King of Macedonia, father of Alexander the Great. The diadem, of papery fine gold, so delicately executed that each myrtle flower's spidery stamens are perfectly distinct, is one of the masterpieces of goldsmithing of all time. It was found in a tomb, many of its 80 leaves and 112 blossoms scattered. Re-assembled, it makes jewelled crowns and diamond tiaras look vulgar and commonplace.

The imperishability of gold treasure, excavated from the earth or retrieved from the sea bed, is its special mystery, so tantalizing it is easy to see why ancient alchemists, searching for an elixir of life, were so certain that gold must enter into the process.

Solid gold was the ultimate sign of wealth but gold leaf, tissue-fine sheets beaten from a nugget of metal and applied to all manner of surfaces, from Pharaonic coffins to Viking roof shingles, seems to have been an early discovery. By the fifteenth century, Cennini is recording that 145 leaves of gold could be beaten out of one Venetian ducat; expert calculations suggest these leaves were comparable with the heaviest modern double-weight gold leaf. For beating out the finest leaves, internal animal membranes were used rather than standard goldbeater's parchment. Powdering gold, for use as a pigment, was difficult, because the particles tended to re-combine under pressure; an amalgam of mercury and gold (poisonous, like so many old formulations) could be rubbed onto metal, or reduced by sieving and heat, to a brittle powder. Later, this was more safely done by grinding fine leaves with honey or salt and washing away any impurities with water.

Cennini's age knew all about extracting the maximum visual impact from applied gold leaf. Water gilding, where loose leaf is applied over a flawless gesso base, and usually burnished subsequently with a dog tooth, or agate, burnisher, gives the most reflective result – as Cennino puts it 'almost dark from its own lustre'. Water gilding, as this skilled, specialized technique is known, is the aristocrat of

The Mirrored Drawing Room created by Gustav III of Sweden in his summer residence, the Haga Pavilion near Stockholm, is one of the most spectacularly beautiful interiors in the world, a dazzling combination of daring design (such delicate glazing embracing such a poetic view) with superb craftsmanship. The decoration, grisaille on water gilding, celebrated the notion of Gustav as Apollo, the sun god, this being his Swedish temple. Gold leaf on furniture, friezes, mirrors, underlines this sunny iconography, warmly radiant even in a cold northern light.

The sheer bravura of gilded bronze ornaments standing out in relief against an elaborately painted background, goes back to a period when craftsmen were not shy of gilding the lily. Ormolu, or bronze, fire-gilt is a very specialised use of gilding, employing poisonous mercury, reserved for the grandest eighteenth- and nineteenth-century (especially Empire) furniture.

metallic finishes, time-consuming, labour-intensive, but instantly distinguishable from any substitute, such as oil gilding (usually on exterior metalwork), silver or tin leaf varnished with a yellow tinted varnish, gold powder or Dutch Metal (brass) artfully distressed over a red base to counterfeit traditional water gilding over red bole. The latter approach is popular today; it is easy, quick and when well-executed a passable imitation of old, worn, dirty gold leaf. It must be said that newly-applied water gilding is almost alarmingly brilliant. Many people genuinely prefer the far cheaper Dutch Metal finish.

All metallic finishes, other than paint or waxes, need some form of adhesive to attach them to the designated surface. In water gilding, the final sizing does the trick. With most other metallic finishes, a varnish-like coating, know as Gold Size, is used, with stated intervals before application. The longer the wait the more brilliant the result, but because of the trickiness of judging the right moment – it varies with climate or room temperature – one recently popular product has been a PVA-based size, which allows an elastic adhesion time of between 20 minutes and 24 hours. Wonderful as this sounds (the product is called Wundasize) experts tell me that the disadvantage is it never fully dries and hardens off once the leaf is applied. Visually this makes little difference but it would affect the durability of the work, especially out of doors.

All that glisters is not gold, as the Bard said, and today there is a wide choice of ersatz

glisters: metallic powders, waxes, in countless shades (silver, copper, endless nuances of gold), paint, spirit, oil- and water-based. Handsome work is done in these, on the principle that whereas one 'fake' metallic finish on its own (cheap gold paint over picture frames is a glaring example) looks artificial, a clever, subtle mixture of all of them can deliver some of the drama of the real thing, especially when used decoratively, as the old japanners did.

Toleware

FOR THE ORIGIN OF TOLE I was driven to my *Petit Larousse Illustré*, a venerable (1910) volume which once belonged to my mother. *Tôle*, from the Old French *taule*, Latin *tabula*, refers to iron or steel *laminé en feuille*, which I take to mean thin sheets of metal laminated, or welded, under pressure. This may have been the definition almost a century ago, but today the word has loosened up, or broadened out, to denote any decoratively painted, highly varnished items in a range of light, thin metal sheet – tin, galvanized aluminium, and so on. Strength, lightness, and a high finish seem to distinguish tolework. A metal base of some sort is necessary too. There is a special appeal about objects – tôle is usually confined to what the glossy magazines call 'accessories' – which combine frivolously pretty decoration with inherent, metallic, lightness-and-toughness, together. The most elegant, and imaginative historical examples of this branch of decorative skill and practice seem to be French, as one might expect, given the name. Anyone visiting (allow two whole days) the Musée des Arts Décoratifs in Paris, will discover a treasury of tole: sconces, trays, candelabra, jardinières, wine coolers. Painted metalware seems to have become fashionable towards the end of the eighteenth century, possibly supplanting to some extent that equally tough, light and malleable material, papier-mâché. The most often seen examples of eighteenth- or nineteenth-century tole tend to be Empire or Directoire in style and decoration, with much gilt decoration and lining, applied to painted background colours, usually dark – black, dark green, mulberry – but occasionally more vivid, such as a sharp chrome yellow. These are always much varnished, to a high, perfect gloss. In many ways toleware seems to be a development of the finishing techniques perfected for the earlier japanning. To begin with, the final effect must have been arrived at in the same way, with many coats of paint and varnish patiently smoothed by hand. Today reproduction tole is factory-sprayed, wherever possible, to speed up the process, giving ideal smoothness, although with some loss of character.

Alongside these salon examples, there also grew up, in the United States especially, a style of tôle decoration which is robustly folk in motifs and colouring. The objects themselves are more domestic, functional – trays, coffee pots, coal buckets. Colours are deeper and warmer – barn red, leaf green are common – and the decoration often reminiscent of German, Austrian or Scandinavian traditional styles, with roses, tendrils, vivid borders in a sort of provincial rococo manner, colourful and charming. Another example of this sort of work, tole for the market-place, would be

Modern reproduction toleware tends to imitate the more upmarket antique, usually French, examples. But it was made and painted, with great verve, in a much more rustic style, as this sturdy, charming early eighteenth-century coffee pot in painted sheet-tin from Massachusetts illustrates. The motifs are perfectly simple, daisy flowers, a scrolled border in the same two colours, but they add colour and fun to a well-made utilitarian piece.

the vividly painted metal wares that were used by canal-boat people, or bargees, until quite recently.

Gilt decoration of leaves, flowers and the like is perhaps the most commonly seen, usually picked out and detailed in black. To begin with, again, gold leaf would have been used, applied over motifs stencilled in gold size, but gradually 'bronze powders' were used, together with or instead of metal leaf. These were cheaper, gave a spectacular powdery soft effect, and could be given a rich look easily by shading gold with silver or copper powders.

Waxes

WHEN ONE EATS A PIECE OF HONEYCOMB, one is effectively eating beeswax along with the honey. Beeswax, which worker bees secrete to build their tiny compartments for storing honey, is by far the most commonly used historically. But there are others – carnauba (exceptionally hard) and candelilla, which are both natural in origin, and paraffin wax, of

It is unusual to find toleware used on a large scale for furniture, so this interesting small Regency commode, in black japanned metal, has a rarity value, as well as being a clever composition in the chinoiserie style, making much use of bronze powders and stencils in the background.

mineral origin and the softest of all. As everyone knows, a thin coating of wax on wood or leather, rubbed energetically (the heat of friction softens the wax and makes it penetrative) brings up a fine, clear gloss which is water-resistant and both seals and protects porous surfaces while gradually filling in the grain and pores of polished wood.

The early Greek and Roman civilizations seem to have used wax as a protective coating on painted surfaces, inside and out, especially over costly vermilion pigment. The result would have acted somewhat like a varnish, enriching colours while giving some protection. Busybody restorers in the nineteenth century waxed frescoes to enliven the colours, quite often with disastrous results. By sealing the porous surface, moisture built up behind and too often a fresco perished from damp.

Encaustic painting, using pigments ground into wax, is today something of a curiosity, though I have read of it being used to stencil over Italian stucco finishes, internally. The effect, as anyone who has tried using stencil crayons will know, is soft and even, easy to control, with no danger of colours bleeding or a sloppy paint smudging or 'creeping'. Ordinary wax crayons are, effectively, pigmented wax – adhesive but crudely uneven in texture when applied. Unsurprisingly, if you think of polishing shoes or furniture, it is heat which smooths and unifies a wax-based pigment. The Romans worked extensively with encaustic, both as a protective measure and for painting on panel. A rigid base panel, rather than a wall, was used, smoothly gessoed to give absorbency and 'tooth'. Colour pigments in wax are applied warm and liquid with a warmed spatula, then burnt in with hot irons passed close to the surface. Successive colour applications could be 'fused' in the same way. Many portraits in encaustic have survived from this period in an excellent state of preservation, there colours unfaded and free of the yellowing that arises on varnished oil painting. Encaustic cannot be varnished, incidentally, since varnish will not adhere to a waxy surface as the photograph here shows wax painting has an intriguing texture.

The unfaded colours and juicy impasto texture of wax painting, or encaustic, show up well on this mummy case portrait from Copenhagen's Ny Carslberg Glyptotek. The mummy cloth was primed first with coats of gesso to give 'tooth' and a smooth white base for painting with tinted wax, used warm.

Brushes

Below: Standard decorating brushes are the basic tools of all paint application. They are designed to cover large areas fast and smoothly. Their springy bristles help to lay off paint without brush marks. They must be cleaned scrupulously after use. A scrubbing brush helps dislodge paint from the stock. Occasional conditioning in brush restorer will prolong their working life.

Above: A hog softener is a very versatile brush used in marbling and graining to soften and blend; for smoothing out colourwash and tinted glazes; and for stippling on small areas, like furniture. The badger softener is the aristocrat. Badger hair, with its naturally occurring split ends, allows the suavest and most subtle manipulation of wet paint and glazes.

Right: Sable brushes are the best possible investment for any decorative painting project where smooth brushwork and fine detail are important and are the professional's choice for performance and longevity. A cheaper alternative is nylon brushes; they cope well with all but the finest brush-work, but are less durable.

Left: A coachliner is used for lining or painting crisp, defining lines on furniture. It has extra long bristles which hold more paint, enabling a line to continue further and more steadily.

Below: Stencil brushes have short bristles and flat or rounded ends and come in several different shapes and sizes. Used in a circular scrubbing movement against a stencil, they produce a soft and precise print.

Far left: A hog fitch is ideal for mixing colours into glazes and paints. *Centre left:* An angle fitch is useful for precise painting up to a line. *Left:* A finishing brush is used for varnishes: it has softish but resilient bristles designed to lessen brushmarks.

Above: A stippling brush is a specialist decorating brush. Used on walls and furniture, it gently lifts off glaze to produce a delicate speckled effect. To achieve a constant pattern the brush should be applied with an even pressure, which may take some practice.

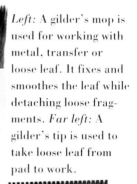

Left: A gilder's mop is used for working with metal, transfer or loose leaf. It fixes and smoothes the leaf while detaching loose fragments. *Far left:* A gilder's tip is used to take loose leaf from pad to work.

Above: A flogger brush has many different uses in professional graining and is fun and easy to use to create woody textures. *Right:* Dragging brushes are used to produce a dragged effect.

Graining combs are effective, easy to use tools which can double for other decorative purposes. *Top:* This is a three-sided rubber comb which combines fine medium and coarse teeth. *Right:* The fine heart grainer is a simple gadget which creates convincing heartwood markings quickly and easily.

Casting Cameos

You will need

■ Old plaster cameos
■ Silicone rubber moulding compound
■ Plaster of Paris (best quality) ■ Shellac
■ Liming wax ■ Soft cloth ■ Manila paper
■ Scalpel ■ Brass picture wire ■ Recess frame ■ Wood glue
■ Decorative paper for mounting ■ Acrylic paint ■ Framer's stapler.

CARVED GEMSTONES, FOR use as seals, date back as far as 5000 BC and were carved in intaglio, that is, hollowed out to act as tiny stamps. Cameos carved in relief, purely decorative, were fashionable in classical Greece and Rome, mounted as jewellery, inset into furniture or simply as exquisite miniature carvings. Antique cameos were collected and new ones commissioned during the Renaissance and later. Most ancient cameos are of onyx or sardonyx; later coral, shell and jet became fashionable. The practice of taking plaster impressions of antique cameos and framing them seems to be an eighteenth-century one.

1 *The key to achieving a good plaster cast is in the creation of a detailed mould. Silicone and rubber solutions are the most effective as they are easy to work with and pick up very fine details. The moulding compounds generally come in two parts: a hardener is added to either a liquid or solid solution and mixed or kneaded thoroughly.*

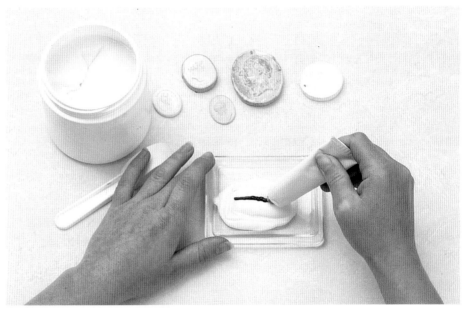

2 *The seal is pressed firmly into the silicone solution. The edges of the mould should be raised slightly above the seal to add depth to the cast. After the mould has set (times vary according to solutions), the original seal is carefully removed.*

3 *Taking care that the mould is stable, plaster of Paris is spooned in. We used a basic plaster of Paris, following the manufacturer's instructions for quantities. A good tip is always to add plaster to water, which should then have the consistency of thick custard.*

4 *The plaster sets fairly quickly, in 15-30 minutes, but the cast is left in the mould for a few hours so that it is not damaged when removed. Uneven edges are tidied up with a scalpel.*

7 *The liming wax is left to dry – the longer it is left, the more 'limed' the appearance. Any excess is then wiped off with a soft cloth, and the seals have taken on a soft, aged look.*

5 *Character is added to the casts by ageing them. A coat of water is brushed liberally over then, and then, using a different brush, they are covered with shellac. We found that a mixture of button polish and white shellac created the ideal colour.*

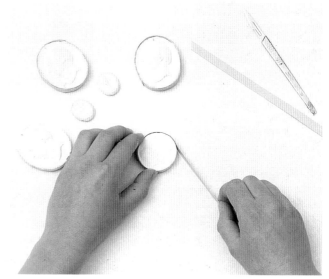

8 *Eighteenth-century seals were usually presented in a frame of dark paper with a gold wire edging. Strips of paper are cut to size – the edge of the paper should come slightly higher than the seal. The strips are then stuck to the seals using ordinary craft glue.*

6 *Although the casts now look more interesting, the effect is rather flat. By applying liming wax, features and details are highlighted. When the shellac is thoroughly dry, the casts are covered with wax, worked into the crevices with a small, stiff brush.*

9 *To edge the seal with gold, we used picture wire. A thin line of glue is spread around the paper rim, then the wire is pressed in place and held for a few minutes.*

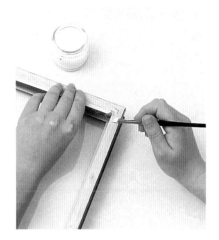

10 The cameos were mounted in a deep recess frame, made to order with slips, glass and the back ready to be fitted together. The backing and slips are covered with decorative paper, the glass dropped into the frame and the covered slips glued to the sides with strong adhesive.

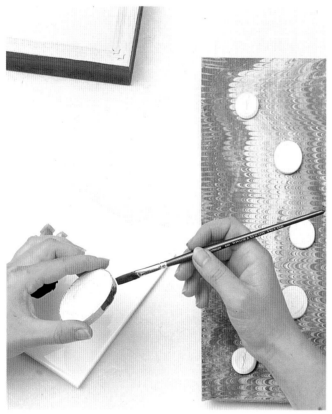

11 The seals are placed onto the background and moved around until the best design is achieved. The paper edges of the seals are matched to the background by picking out a colour and painting. The seals are glued to the background with wood glue and pressed firmly for a few minutes. The mounted seals and backing board are dropped into the frame and stapled all round.

Twin examples of framed and mounted cameos on a marbled paper in mahogany recessed frames. This relatively austere treatment is typically of the eighteenth and nineteenth centuries, when such collections would have been displayed in a study, cabinet of curiosities or possibly a library. They were kept more as reminders of their antique originals, for the scholarly eye, than as decorative objects in themselves, though the latter is more likely to be their appeal today. Antique dealers have begun re-casting these attractive miniatures. They also look excellent mounted on paper made from copper-plate documents enlarged on a photocopier.

Water Gilding

The subject we chose for this project was a wooden picture frame, genuinely antique, but with a battered grey painted finish. Considerable filling was needed to level up the scars, while the paint had to be fiercely sanded to get back to a decent surface. Painstaking gessoing brought it to a china-smooth finish, and genuine gold leaf completed the transformation, emphasizing the frame's simple but elegant moulding. The project took four books of loose gold leaf (Perse, 22.3ct, a slightly reddish gold), so the materials alone were not cheap, and the cost in time was considerable, though with practice this speeds up. Water gilding is strikingly beautiful, but demands fierce concentration and perfectionism and consecutive actions. It is a vocation rather than a spare-time hobby.

You will need

■ Wet-and-dry abrasive paper ■ *Bain marie* (double boiler) ■ Sieve ■ Rabbit skin glue granules ■ Whiting ■ Soft brush ■ Yellow clay ■ Red clay ■ Wire wool ■ Gilder's pad ■ Gilder's knife ■ Gilder's tip ■ Loose gold leaf ■ Methylated spirits (denatured alcohol) ■ Cotton wool balls ■ Agate burnisher

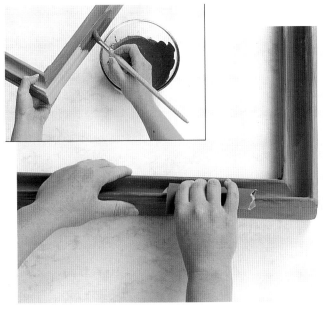

1 Apply a coat of clearcole and leave to dry overnight. This is followed by 6-12 coats of gesso brushed on in opposite directions to each other, sanding between coats. Then 1 coat of yellow clay and 2 coats of red clay, again sanding between coats.

2 When completely dry, use wet-and-dry paper and wire wool to polish the clay to a dark, shiny surface. Using a soft brush cover the clay with a coat of methylated spirits. This will de-grease the surface, removing any dust or dirt in preparation for gilding.

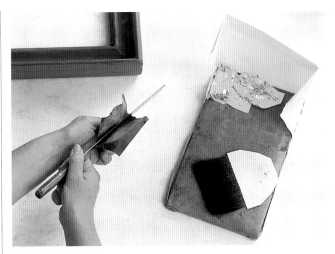

3 Now prepare your gilding instruments. Using a piece of wet-and-dry paper briskly run it along the surface of the knife to remove any grease or dirt. Open the book of gold leaf and gently blow about 4-5 pieces into the back of the gilder's pad.

4 For the gold leaf to adhere to the frame a solution of gilding water must be liberally brushed onto the surface. This is prepared by adding methylated spirits to water until the liquid changes colour, then adding a teaspoon of melted rabbit skin size.

5 *Using the knife, cut a piece of gold leaf to size. Pick up with the tip; rub the tip across your neck to help it adhere. Thoroughly cover surface with gilder's water then place leaf onto the frame.*

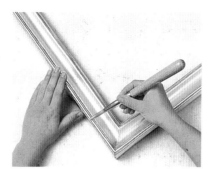

6 *After a few minutes, press down on the leaf with cotton wool to remove excess gilding water. After about an hour, when the gold is dry, burnish the edges of the frame with an agate burnisher.*

RECIPES

Yellow clay Add 1 part water to 1 part of melted rabbit skin size and enough yellow clay to give a creamy consistency.

Red clay As above but add 2 parts rabbit skin size to 1 part water.

Basic rabbit-skin size Add 50g of rabbit-skin size granules to 550ml of water, leave overnight to feather up. Melt the solution in a *bain marie* until all the granules have dissolved; do not allow mixture to boil.

Clearcole (first coat of gesso) Melt 1 part rabbit-skin size with 1 part water in a *bain marie* and sieve in enough whiting to colour the mixture. When painted onto the frame the mixture should appear translucent.

Gesso Add 1 part water to 2 parts of melted rabbit-skin size. Sieve whiting into the mixture and stir with a large brush in a *bain marie* until it takes on the consistency of thick emulsion. Do not allow to boil as this will weaken the strength. Try to keep mixture warm while using.

Japanning and Gilding a Box

THE POINT OF DEPARTURE FOR this project was a plain wooden box, decently made, a relic from the days when cigarettes were not politically incorrect. Japanning is too time-consuming to waste on anything flimsy, so check the construction: hinges must work and the wood must be solid, not veneered. We wanted a contemporary design incorporating the rare, deep, vivid blue of period japanned pieces. Gilding is a natural partner, adding warmth and richness. We used a fast technique – transfer Dutch Metal (in fact, brass leaf) over traditional japan size. Experience has convinced me that the pure brilliance of real gold leaf (see page 158) applied in the traditional way is wasted on a japanned item. Finishing coats of shellac bury the true quality of the metallic finish. Much as we liked the clean contrast of gilded rectangles with blue japan, we realized, too late, that gilded raised work in japanning needs to be rounded rather than crisply bevelled because the patient smoothing and rubbing back tends to damage sharp edges. The solution, to rub *round* the gilding, prevented the broad sweeping abrasion that yields the desired flawless smoothness.

You will need

■ Gesso ■ Tracing paper, pencil, ruler and scalpel ■ Fine-grade wet-and-dry abrasive paper ■ Shellac ■ Acrylic colours in ultramarine and red/brown or red bole ■ Gilder's japan size ■ Transfer Dutch Metal ■ Bleached shellac and methylated spirits (denatured alcohol) ■ Soap ■ Rottenstone

1 *Here shapes for the applied raised gilt work are drawn on tracing paper. Laid over the gessoed box, they give an ida of the final effect and indicate spacing.*

2 *The next step is to cut out the rectangles, drop them in place and mark them out in pencil, checking with a ruler that they are correctly aligned.*

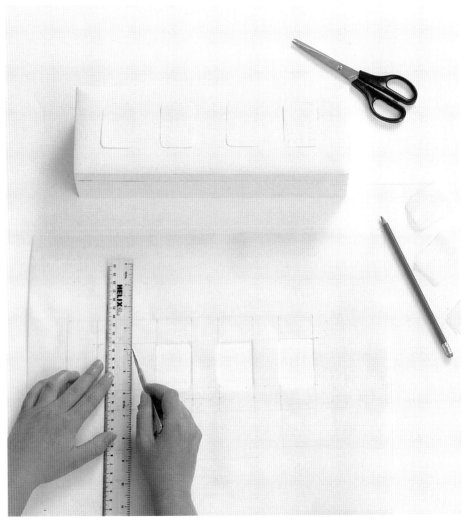

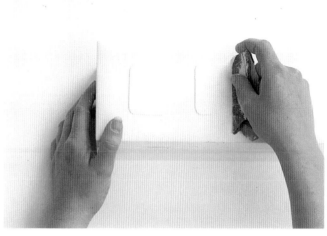

3 *Raising the pencilled rectangles is done with layer after layer of traditional gesso, applied with a fine brush for tidy edges and a fatter, soft one for infilling. Acrylic gesso would speed this up but is more expensive and less responsive and fine-textured when it comes to smoothing.*

4 *Smoothing back the gesso requires fine grade wet-and-dry abrasive paper, used sensitively to keep the crisp bevelled edges sharp. Fold the paper and scrape with a light hand, although firmness is also needed to compact the gesso well.*

5 *Several coats of acrylic/casein colour in a rich ultramarine are brushed over the surrounding areas. They were first sealed with a coat of standard shellac to prevent the colour being swallowed up unevenly by the porous gesso.*

6 *Raised gesso rectangles, first primed with a red-brown acrylic paint in imitation of gilder's bole, are brushed over with gilder's japan size. When the size is ideally 'tacky', it should 'click' when rapped with a knuckle.*

7 A long-awaited moment, when the 'transfer leaf' is pressed down onto the sized rectangles. The tacky size grips the metal leaf, while rubbing with fingers on the waxed paper backing ensures a clean adhesion. This can be seen clearly.

8 After the leaf has settled overnight, loose 'bits' are wiped off with cotton wool in preparation for japanning itself. Many coats of bleached shellac, slightly thinned with methylated spirit, are brushed over the painted surfaces, each coat at right angles to the one before to lessen brushmarks. Much smoothing in between, too.

9 The smoothing process, using wet-and-dry paper wiped over a cake of soap for lubrication. This abrasion is critical to a japanned finish – levelling, removing any grit or dust that settles on drying varnish, giving a soft polished lustre rather than a glitzy shellac shine.

The final *objet de luxe*, transformed with colour, gilt and elbowgrease, holding its own among other painted surfaces. If you want to make something extraordinary and deliciously tactile, japanning is a technique to work with. But allow time – this is a labour of love.

10 Moistened rottenstone powder is rubbed over the japanned finish with a soft rag. This has a fine cutting action on the built-up shellac and adds further to the ideal tactile smoothness of a japanned piece.

Waxing Wood

WAXES AND WOOD DO SEEM to have a natural affinity. As well as enriching the woods natural colour, and contributing to its shine by filling the grain and pores, wax brings up the natural figuring in a subtle, sympathetic way. However, as all the old cabinetmakers were well aware, it is the elbow-grease in patient rubbing over a long time that finally yields the deep patina one admires on antique pieces. But waxes need not be woody coloured. Liming wax, a soft wax containing titanium white pigment, is an easy way to achieve the fashionably 'greyed' look of limed wood, best on hardwoods like oak and ash though it can be used on pine too. Coloured waxes are a fun way of tinting light wood without obscuring the grain.

You will need

■ Sponge ■ Wire brush
■ Paint Magic Wood-
wash, Slate ■ Soft
cloths ■ Wire wool

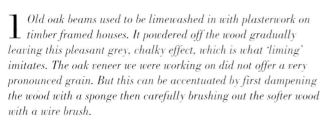

2 *Liming works equally well on stripped, bare or stained wood. We choose to colour our oak veneer with a green woodwash. This was diluted with water, so as not to conceal the grain, then rubbed over the oak with a cloth.*

1 *Old oak beams used to be limewashed in with plasterwork on timber framed houses. It powdered off the wood gradually leaving this pleasant grey, chalky effect, which is what 'liming' imitates. The oak veneer we were working on did not offer a very pronounced grain. But this can be accentuated by first dampening the wood with a sponge then carefully brushing out the softer wood with a wire brush.*

3 *When diluted as per the recommended quantities, 1 part paint to 2 parts water, the woodwash should take approximately 15 minutes to dry. Then useing wirewool generously apply a coat of liming wax. Work into and against the grain then leave to dry for approximately 30 minutes.*

4 *Remove the excess liming wax with a piece of wirewool or a cloth; this should produce a soft whitened effect. Conservators sometimes limewash exterior oak beams, wire brushing them after a few days to get this effect.*

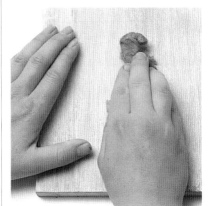

Antiquing wax
Antiquing wax is a natural looking way of intensifying the colour of pale wood. It can be used on its own or over a stain. Rub the wax really hard, to force it into the grain preventing stickiness and producing a deep shine.

Coloured wax
Coloured waxes can be used along with stains, paints etc. to get a variety of effects. Used with discretion, in a similar way to antiquing wax, this wax gives soft, rich colour with a silky texture without obscuring the wood grain.

The samples shown here were all oak veneered plywood, in the natural pale colour of American oak, a light biscuit colour untreated. The grain is much less pronounced than it would be on European oak, and being a veneer rather than hardwood, 'clearing' the grain for liming neds to proceed cautiously, so as not to cut through the veneer itself. Antiquing wax (*top*) is a dark tinted wax which adds depth of colour as well as shine. It is popular with antique dealers too for use over painted pieces, where it has a mellowing efect on colours without being too shiny. Liming wax over a green woodwash (*centre*) gives the same wood a sophisticated 'greyed' finish, quickly and easily. Coloured wax (*below*) is a new idea, giving an interesting transparent tint to pale wood which can look very rich and feels delicious to touch. See Howard Raybould's folding mirror on page 103.

Crackle Glaze

CRACKLE GLAZE, A TRANSPARENT varnish-type proprietary product, provides an ideally fast and simple route to the 'heavily distressed' effect currently popular for painted furniture. The glaze is applied between two coats of standard water-based emulsion (latex) paints. As soon as the moisture in the top coat of paint connects with the water-activated glaze, this starts cracking up, along with the top coat of paint, to give the 'alligatoring' effect used as a decorative finish in its own right or as a distressing technique for antiquing purposes. Crackling is most dramatic when the paint colours are strongly contrasting, as here. Dark colours over metallic paints look handsome. Subtle tone-on-tone combinations, such as oyster on white, are more sophisticated. Crackled surfaces *must* be sealed with oil- or spirit-, not water-based varnish.

You will need

- Two water-based paints in contrasting colours ■ Crackle glaze ■ Oil based matt varnish or shellac ■ Antiquing wax and a soft cloth ■ Decorators or varnishing brushes small and large

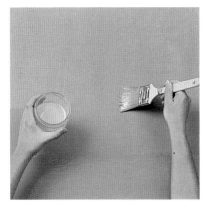

1 The crackle glaze is brushed over the dry base coat, here a bright green, using a standard varnish brush. It should cover the whole surface, bearing in mind that the final 'crackling' follows the direction of the brushstrokes. The thicker the glaze coat, the larger the cracks.

2 Use a larger brush to apply red top colour, after the glaze is dry. Brush paint on evenly but thickly, to cover base. Do not go back over surfaces after the 'crackling' begins: this results in a messy smear. Brushing top coat at right angles to glaze gives regular 'checks'; in the same direction it gives dramatic fissures.

3 Cracks begin appearing within a minute, and continue opening up until the top coat is dry. Training a hair dryer on the surface gives a more emphatic crackle. A coat of tinted antiquing wax gives a rich pattern and softens brightly contrasting colours.

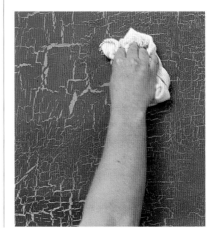

4 Rub off any excess wax and when quite dry, seal with a coat of oil-based matt varnish or shellac. Water-based varnish would re-activate the glaze. Over paper shades, use a clear wax instead. As many as five coats, buffed with a soft clean cloth, create a mellow surface, flattering to old country furniture.

Crackled in barn red over bright green, and deeply waxed, this rustic corner cupboard shows how attractive this finish can look, fittting in comfortably with colourful kitchen clutter. Where possible, lay pieces flat so the process can done on a horizontal surface, unscrewing doors if necessary. This cuts the risk of sags occurring as the top coat begins to move.

Notes and Recipes

Maestro Giacomo's
Stucco Lustro

The old stuccoists also call this 'encaustic', because of the use of beeswax. I give the recipe for the reader's interest; our attempts with it were only partially successful. Success depends crucially on smooth compacting of the stucco base, applying many fine layers of the wax coat, and careful use of heat at the end to flatten and make shiny without scorching the wax.

Over a smooth base of plaster made with one part mature putty lime to two parts fine sharp sand, an undercoat is applied. This is made from one part strong rabbit skin size, one part boiled linseed oil, one part white spirit, two parts white marble dust and one part zinc white.

This is applied thinly, with firm pressure, over the whole surface and smoothed out well with a float or trowel. When dry it is rubbed down with fine wet-and-dry paper, until a porcelain-smooth finish is achieved.

When this is quite dry, a paste is applied very thinly over the surface using a metal spatula, with enough force to heat the tool. The Maestro adds pigment to the wax paste. We felt it would be better to tint the undercoat as well. The paste is made as follows: four parts beeswax, five parts boiled linseed oil and four parts oil of turpentine.

The pigment to be added is dissolved in a little raw linseed oil. The paste, which is quite firm, is scraped very thinly over the surface with the spatula in a downward cross-hatching style. The need for super-smoothness is essential here because the wax/pigment mixture must glide on evenly and penentrate the undercoat. Many thin layers are applied.

Polishing is done in one of three ways: by rubbing firmly with a hot (but not too hot) iron; by carefully passing heat from a distance across the surface to soften the wax (a hot air stripper or blowtorch can be used), then polishing with a cold iron; or by using the iron without additional heat, but so vigorously that the friction that is generated warms and softens the encaustic. The irons used by professional stuccoists are wooden-handled, not unlike plasterers' trowels in profile, but with a flat, heavy metal base. They must be perfectly smooth and clean, so as not to rip or scratch the encaustic. We used an antique flatiron with some success.

Note: A perfect base is the key to success with this stucco lustro finish. Dips or hollows that the iron cannot reach when polishing will show up against the brilliantly shiny surrounding work.

Marmorino

For a coloured, polished marmorino the recipe is as follows: the first or 'pricking up' coat consists of one part mature putty lime to two parts coarse sharp sand. Second and third coats are made up with one part putty lime to one part marble dust. Colour is added to both these coats with dry pigment dissolved in water. A small added quantity of boiled linseed oil helps to disperse colour smoothly. The first of these coats is 2mm thick and well-smoothed; the second is 1mm thick and should be applied with pressure for maximum smoothness.

When this is thoroughly dry, it is brushed over with a sealing/polishing soap finish, made as follows:

One bar of pure olive oil *savon de Marseille* is chopped and added to 10 litres of water, and the mixture is heated very gently until the soap melts. This is then mixed with 3 kg of leftover marmorino and stirred up thoroughly. After 48 hours the mixture will have separated into a soapy liquid with the lime settled out at the bottom. The froth is skimmed off and discarded. The remaining liquid is poured off and brushed over the dry marmorino. The first coat is applied horizontally and the second (after the first coat has dried) vertically. As the soap/lime mix dries the surface goes dull and slightly chalky. When the marmorino has dried out thoroughly, the whole surface is polished either by hand with soft woollen cloths or a lambs-wool pad on a power drill.

Note: By using coloured marble dust instead of pigment a very even, integrated surface can be achieved, but colours will be pale.

Stucco – a Historical Recipe*

Three parts of putty lime are mixed with two parts of fine washed sand or marble dust to which a small amount of plaster of Paris is added to prevent cracking.

Stucco – a Modern Recipe for Exterior Work

One part white Portland Cement to two to three parts of marble dust, white sand, crushed quartz or limestone.

Sand: Vitruvius, the Roman writer, advised this test for the cleanness of sharp sand: throw it onto a white cloth and then shake it out; if the cloth is not soiled and no dirt has adhered to it then the sand is suitable.

A well-graded sharp sand is one where particles are angular but varied in size. Less cement is needed to bind well-graded sand into a strong mortar or render, because particles interlock.

Rough Cast Exterior Finish

Known as harling in Scotland, this is a traditional weather-proofing device. First a 'pricking up' coat of lime, sand and hair is applied. When this is nearly dry, a second coat is applied and washed gravel mixed with limewash is thrown hard enough at the surface to embed the gravel in the still-pliant render.

To Harden Plaster Casts*

Plaster casts may be rendered hard by brushing on a hot solution of alum or by soaking in raw linseed oil for ten hours.

Plaster Notes

Any of the following can be used to polish lime plaster: pure soap, pure white beeswax, paraffin wax or French chalk. To retard setting, add dilute size, ammonia or stale beer.

Keene's Cement

A patent cement no longer in production but useful for anyone contemplating making scagliola to know about.

Lump gypsum is calcined at a high temperature until anhydrous, then ground. Accelerators such as alum, potash or salt are added. Unlike retarded plasters which harden at spaced points and gradually connect up, Keene's cement hardens at an equal rate throughout. It keeps better than semi-hydrated plaster, it can be made plastic again after the initial set and it takes a good polish.

Alternative recipe for Scagliola

Pure gypsum plaster with isinglass or animal glue added.

Parge

As well as lime, sand, hair and straw, old recipes for parge included fresh cow dung and horse's urine, mixed together until tough and leathery.

Compo Recipe*

Two and a half pounds of pearl glue is steeped in water and melted over heat. A pint of linseed oil and two pounds of resin are blended separately and added to the liquid glue. Whiting is then sifted into the mixture until a doughy consistency is reached. The ingredients are mixed, rolled, kneaded and beaten to make a smooth tough elastic putty, which is steamed to make it pliable for use. To cast, oil is smeared over a boxwood mould. This is filled until it is half an inch 'proud' with compo, then covered with a board and put into a screw-type press.

(This recipe is quoted without having been tested, so the quantities have not been checked or metricated.)

* From *Plastering Plain and Decorative* by W Millar (see **Bibliography,** p.173).

List of Suppliers

ARTIST'S MATERIALS

Paint Magic Head Office
(Contact for nearest branch)
79 Shepperton Road
Islington
London
N1 3DF
Tel: 0171 354 9696
Pigments, varnishes, brushes, stencils –
mail order

J W Bollom
121 South Liberty Lane
Ashton Vale
Bristol
Tel: 01179 665151
Glazes, varnishes, tinting colours and paints

L Cornelissen & Son Ltd
105 Great Russell Street
London
WC1B 3RY
Tel: 0171 636 1045
Materials for painters, pastellists, gilders
and printmakers – mail order

Craig and Rose Plc
172 Leith Walk
Edinburgh
EH6 5EB
Tel: 0131 554 1131
Oils, glazes, varnishes – mail order

Foxell & James Ltd
57 Farringdon Road
London
EC1M 3JB
Tel: 0171 405 0152
Woodfinishes, paints, restoration products -
mail order

W Habberley Meadows
5 Saxon Way
Chelmsley Wood
Birmingham
B37 5AY
Tel: 0121 770 2905
Gilding and artist's materials

Nutshell Natural Paints
Newtake
Staverton
Devon
TQ9 6PE
Tel: 01803 762329
Earth and mineral pigments, paints,
varnishes, waxes – mail order only

Papers and Paints
4 Park Walk
London
SW10 0AD
Tel: 0171 352 8626
Historic paints, matched glazes, stencils –
mail order

Stuart R Stevenson
68 Clerkenwell Road
London
EC1M 5QA
Tel: 0171 253 1693
Artist's and gilding materials – mail order

TILE AND CERAMIC SUPPLIERS

Ceramatech Ltd.
Unit 16 Frontier Works
33 Queen Street
London
N17 8JA
Tel: 0181 885 4492
Ceramic and pottery materials – mail order

Ceramic Creations
40A Trading Estate
Okus Road
Swindon
SN1 4JI
Tel: 01793 431837
Ceramic materials – mail order

Hobby Ceramic Supplies
2 St Leonards Road
Forres
Morayshire
IV36 0DN
Tel: 01309 672987

M.G.A. Chingford
188-192 Chingford Mount Road
London
E4 8JR
Tel: 0181 524 0924
Wall and floor tile distributors – mail order

SPECIALISTS

Cole & Son (Wallpapers) Ltd
144 Offord Road
London
N1 1NS
Tel: 0171 607 4288
Hand-blocked wallpapers, fabrics &
special paint colours – mail order

The Frame Factory
20 Cross Street
Islington
London
N1 2BG
Tel: 0171 354 3134
Frames made to order; also at
159 Haverstock Hill
London
NW3 4QT
Tel: 0171 483 2050
296 Streatham High Road
London
SW16 6HG
Tel: 0181 677 1882

Falkiner Fine Papers Ltd.
76 Southampton Row
London
WC1B 4AR
Tel: 0171 831 1151
Specialist papers

Alec Tiranti Ltd
27 Warren Street
London
W1P 5DG
Tel: 0171 636 8565
Sculpting and moulding supplies – mail
order

LIME MATERIALS

H J Chard & Sons
Albert Road
Totterdown Bridge
Bristol
Avon
BS2 0XS
Tel: 01179 777681
Lime and building materials – mail order

Liz and Bruce Induni
11 Park Road
Swanage
Dorset BH19 2AA
Tel: 01924 423274
Limewash, distemper and pigments

Hirst Conservation Materials Ltd.
Laughton
Near Sleaford
Lincolnshire
NG34 0HE
Tel: 01529 497517
Lime and traditional building materials –
mail order

Masons Mortar
61-67 Trafalgar Lane
Edinburgh
EH6 4DQ
Tel: 0131 555 0503
Lime and conservation materials – mail
order

Jane Schofield
Lewdon Farm
Black Dog
Crediton
Devon
EX17 4QQ
Tel: 01884 861181
Lime and conservation materials – mail
order

BUILDING MATERIALS

Bowman Brothers, A Cohen
61-63 Cowcross Street
West Smithfield
London
EC1M 6BP
Tel: 0171 253 5892

MOSAIC MATERIALS

Paul Fricker Ltd.
Well Park
Willeys Avenue
Exeter
Devon
EX2 8BE
Tel: 01392 78636
Mosaics and materials

MCC Mosaics
2A Larches Avenue
London
SW14 8LX
Tel: 0973 452962
Mosaics – mail order

Edgar Udny & Co. Ltd.
314 Balham High Road
London
SW17 7AA
Tel: 0181 767 8181
Mosaic tools and materials – mail order

OVERSEAS SUPPLIERS

Paint Magic Stores:
Paint Magic San Francisco
2426 Fillmore Street
San Francisco CA 94115
USA
Tel: 415 292 7780

Paint Magic Calgary
101, 1019 17th Avenue S.W.
Calgary
Alverta T2T0A7
Canada
Tel: 403 245 6866

Paint Magic Singapore
30 Watten Rise
Singapore 1128
Tel: 65 463 1981

USA

A range of Paint Magic supplies are also
available from 'Pottery Barn' shops around
the USA:
Pottery Barn
262 Plaza Frontenac
St Louis
Mo 63131
USA
Tel: 314 569 3532

Pottery Barn
Highland Village
4011 Westheimer Road
Houston
TX 77027
USA
Tel: 619 296 8014

Pottery Barn
590 Fashion Valley Drive
San Diego
CA 92108
USA
Tel: 619 296 8014

American Mosaic Company
912 First Street NW
Washington DC 20001
USA
Tel: 301 773 2800

Mosaic Supplies
Janovic/Plaza, Inc.
30-35 Thomson Avenue
Long Island City, NY 11101
USA
Tel: 718 392 3999

Artists materials
Sepp Leaf
381 Park Avenue South
New York
NY 10016
USA
Tel: 212 683 2840

Gold leaf and gilding supplies
Vedovato Brothers Inc
246 East 116 Street
New York
NY 10029 USA
Tel: 212 534 2854
Mosaic supplies

CANADA

Gemst Inc.
5380 Sherbrooke West
Montreal
Quebec
Canada
H4A 1V6
Tel: 514 488 5104
Artists materials

AUSTRALIA

Bristol Decorator Centre
76 Oatley Court
Belconnen
Australia
ACT 2617
Tel:6 253 2
Paints and decorators' supplies

Camden Art
188-200 Gertrude Street
Fitzroy
Victoria
Australia 3065
9 416 1680
Mosaic supplies

Bibliography

Adam, Peter, EILEEN GRAY, ARCHITECT DESIGNER
Thames and Hudson, London, 1987

Baker, Mel, THE SKILLS OF PLASTERING
Macmillan, London, 1990

Barrucand, Marianne and Bednorz, Achim, MOORISH ARCHITECTURE
IN ANDULUCIA
Taschen, Cologne, 1992

Beacham, Peter (ed.), DEVON BUILDINGS, AN INTRODUCTION TO
LOCAL TRADITIONS,
Devon Books, Devon, 1990

Beard, Geoffrey, CRAFTSMEN AND INTERIOR DECORATION IN
ENGLAND 1660-1820
Bloomsbury Books, London, 1986

Binski, Paul, MEDIEVAL CRAFTSMEN, PAINTERS,
British Museum Press, London, 1991

Boase, T.S.R., GIORGIO VASARI THE MAN AND THE BOOK
Princeton University Press, Princeton, 1979

Bomford, David, et al, ART IN THE MAKING -
ITALIAN PAINTING BEFORE 1400
The National Gallery, London, 1989

Bourne, Jonathan, et al, LACQUER, AN INTERNATIONAL HISTORY
AND COLLECTORS GUIDE,
Bracken Books, London, 1989

Cennini, Cennino d'Andrea, THE CRAFTSMAN'S HANDBOOK (*IL
LIBRO DELL' ARTE*)
trans. Thompson Jr, Daniel V,
Dover Publication Inc., NY, 1954

Davey, Norman, A HISTORY OF BUILDING MATERIALS,
Phoenix House, London, 1961

Doerner, Max, THE MATERIALS OF THE ARTIST,
trans., Neuhaus, Eugen
Hart-Davis MacGibbon, London, 1969

Garner, Sir Harry, CHINESE LACQUER,
Faber and Faber Ltd., London, 1979

Goodwin, Arthur, THE TECHNIQUE OF MOSAIC,
Batsford, London, 1985

Goodwin, Elaine.M,DECORATIVE MOSAICS,
Charles Letts & Co. Ltd, London, 1992

Headley, Gwyn and Meulenkamp, Wim, FOLLIES - A GUIDE TO
ROGUE ARCHITECTURE IN ENGLAND, SCOTLAND AND WALES
Jonathan Cape, London, 1990

Hill, Derek and Grahar, Oleg, ISLAMIC ARCHITECTURE AND ITS
DECORATION, A.D. 800-1500, 2nd Edition,
Faber and Faber, London, 1967

Hill, Neville, et al., LIME AND OTHER ALTERNATIVE CEMENTS
Intermediate Technology Publications, London, 1992

Hooker, Denise, (ed.), ART OF THE WESTERN WORLD
Boxtree Ltd., London, 1991

Jacobson, Dawn, CHINOISERIE
Phaidon Press Ltd, London, 1993

James,T.G.H., EGYPTIAN PAINTING
British Museum Press, London, 1985

Killen, Geoffrey, EGYPTIAN WOODWORKING AND FURNITURE
Shire Publications, Princes Risborough, 1994

LIME NEWS, (MORTAR ISSUE)
The Building Limes Forum, Woodstock, October 1994

Ling, Roger, ROMAN PAINTING
CUP, Cambridge, 1991

Manning, Hiram, MANNING ON DECOUPAGE
Dover Publications, Inc, NY, 1980

Massey, Robert, FORMULAS FOR PAINTERS
Watson Guptill, N.Y., 1979

Mayer, Ralph, DICTIONARY OF ART TERMS AND TECHNIQUES
Collins and Brown, London, 1993

Merrifield (Mrs), THE ART OF FRESCO PAINTING
Tiranti, London, 1952

Millar, W, PLASTERING PLAIN AND DECORATIVE
Batsford, London, 1927

Murphy, Richard, CARLO SCARPA AND THE CASTELVECCHIO
Butterworth Architecture, London 1990

Quarnetti, Gilberto, *I QUADERNI DI GIACOMO QUERINI DA VENEZIA*
1889
Reprinted Medolago, date unknown

Sloan, Annie and Gwynn, Kate, TRADITIONAL PAINTS AND FINISHES
Collins and Brown, London, 1993

Taylor, J.B., PLASTERING, 5th Edition
Longman Scientific & Technical, Harlow, 1990

Thompson, Daniel.V., MATERIALS AND TECHNIQUES OF MEDIEVAL
PAINTING
Dover Publications Inc., NY, 1956

Titian, Rodrigo and Rosario, GILDING AND LACQUERING
Charles Letts & Co Ltd, London, 1993

Verrall, W., THE MODERN PLASTERER
Caxton Publishing Company Ltd, London
Date unknown, c. 1930s

VITRUVIUS, THE TEN BOOKS ON ARCHITECTURE
trans., Hicky Morgan, Morris,
Dover Publications Inc., NY 1960

Walker, Susan, ROMAN ART
British Museum Press, London, 1991

Watkin, David, THE ROYAL INTERIORS OF REGENCY ENGLAND
J M Dent & Sons Ltd., London, 1984

Index

Author's Acknowledgments

This book could not have happened without a great deal of help, involvement and forebearance on the part of very many people, to all of whom I remain deeply indebted: to my publishing team at Weidenfeld & Nicolson first of all for supporting an idea which took shape gradually, moving in unexpected directions. Michael Dover and Gabrielle Townsend provided helpful guidelines. Judy Spours did noble and exemplary work editing my overflowing text seamlessly. Rona Skene was brilliant in finding appropriate and exciting pictures and Steve Wooster designed page layouts which convey information dynamically while being a pleasure to look at.

Busy professional people were unstintingly generous with time, advice, photographs. My warmest thanks are due to the following architects: John Outram, Richard Murphy, Richard MacCormac, Stefan Buzas, Luigi Croce. Then there were the people who helped my research into the complexities of building limes: Peter Hood, Bob Bennett, Liz Induni, Jane Schofield, and Nicola Sperry of the SPAB who kindly lent me back numbers of Lime News

Other specialists in different fields contributed valuable information and a few trade secrets to boot. For shellwork, Diana Reynell and Peter Coke. For mosaic, Chris Skinner, Celia Gregory, Martin Cohen, Jody Clarke of MCC Mosaics and Ann Hughes of Mosaik. For pebble mosaic, Maggie Howarth and Tim Coppard. For fibrous plaster, dear Mr Butcher of Butchers Plastering. Our concrete experts ranged from Gordon Whitwell of Histon Concrete to the clever team of McCollin Bryan whose concrete clock provided one of our strongest images. Alexandra Artley and Charles Hemmings did clear, beautiful work on the complex subject of historic colour in such fascinating detail.

For ceramic knowhow I am grateful to Steve Rafferty of Ceramatech, for materials and assistance, and especially to Trish Phillips of the Sir John Cass Institute and Kim Ng, her star pupil, who helped us decode the mysteries of a kiln lent by my neighbour and old friend, artist Polly Hope. Gilding and painting finishes: here our expert was Liza Shamash, as charming as she is talented, and Thandi McPherson who painted walls and cupboards without turning a hair.

Complete strangers generously allowed us to photograph their homes. These include the artist Robert Organ; Jonathan Hyde and Isobel Buchanan, Kevin McCabe, Spencer Swaffer and Freya Robins in Arundel. And not a stranger – my daughter, Daisy Goodwin, to whom a special hug and thank-you.

Who more informed about trade secrets than tradespeople? In this special category I would like to thank the endlessly helpful Stuart Stevenson, Patrick Ball of Cole & Son Wallpapers and Patrick Baty of Papers and Paints.

Thanks also to Ben Rye and Peter Maynard for their obliging help and to Jennifer Spark and Joey Hardy for routing out information.

Photographers become part of the working family, with vital input to the buzz and style of an illustrated book. David George drove hundreds of miles to catch some of the 'special effects' recorded here, always using natural light. Mark Gatehouse kept his cool and control, over studio photography and location work of the most cliff-hanging sort, and allowed us to pack his studio floor with sudden 'no-go' areas. They picked up the spirit of the undertaking with an enthusiasm and skill which I award special Brownie points for. And a special Brownie badge should go to Peter Townsend, an amateur, but whose crisp and lively pictures of flint, pargeting, etc, have handsomely filled a real gap in the book.

The 'home team', as I think of them, were absolutely invaluable and their dedication went well beyond a job remit. They pushed ahead with hands-on projects while I fought with typewriter and fax machine. Sarah Curran, formerly of Sotheby's, calmly progressed a whole swathe of disparate undertakings, prompt, bright and together always, a PA to die for. Craig Emerson and Tom Lane took on tricky lime plastering assignments, viz marmorino, with enthusiasm and a proper degree of analytical interest, helping make sense of centuries-old recipes, looking up old books in museum libraries, mixing till their arms ached.

And finally, my thanks are due to the entire staff of Paint Magic, for respecting my headlong commitment to a new book, holding back on faxes, postponing meetings and generally helping me meet a red-hot deadline. So my last sincere thanks to Charles, Angie, Sarah, Helen, Chloe, Jason, Hamish and more besides for letting me do my own thing, graciously.

Photographic Acknowledgements

All photographs are by Mark Gatehouse or David George except as stated below.
6 EWA/Tim Street-Porter; 8 Contemporary Applied Arts; 9 Interior World/Christopher Simon Sykes; 12-13 RHPL; 14 Hutchinson Library; 16 Francesco Venturi/KEA; 17-19 Peter Townsend; 20 John Outram; 21 left Peter Cook, MJP Architects; 21 right Arcaid/Richard Bryant; 22 National Trust Picture Library/J Whitaker; 23 Interior World/Christopher Simon Sykes; 25 Richard Murphy; 26-27 Francesco Venturi/KEA; 28 Arcaid/Jeremy Cockayne; 29 World of Interiors/Philip Sayer; 30-31 Christie's Colour Library; 32 Bildarchiv Preussischer Kulturbesitz, Berlin; 33 Interior World/Christopher Simon Sykes; 37 below Interior World; 54-55 SCALA, Florence; 56 left Maggie Howarth; 56 right Francesco Venturi/KEA; 57; Francesco Venturi/KEA; 58 SCALA, Florence; 59 Sonia Halliday Photographs; 60 RHPL; 61-63 Francesco Venturi/KEA; 64 RHPL; 65 Arcaid/Richard Bryant; 68-69 National Trust Photo Library/Christopher Hurst; 70 Christie's Colour Library; 71 Christie's Colour LIbrary; 88-9 Arcaid/Mark Fiennes; 90 Francesco Venturi/KEA; 91 BAL; 92,93 RHPL; 95 Lars Hallen/Design Press; 96 Arcaid/David Fowler; 97 Cassells/EWA; 98 Sonia Halliday Photos; 99 SCALA, Florence; 100-101 Robert Harding Syndication/Women's Journal; 102 RHPL; 103 Contemporary Applied Arts; 112 Interior World/Fritz von der Schulenburg;113 Pallant House, Chichester; 114 National Motor Museum, Beaulieu; 115 RHPL; 134-5 BAL/Mallet and Son Antiques; 140 Trustees of Victoria and Albert Museum, London; 141 Interior World/Fritz von der Schulenburg; 142, 143 BAL/Russell Cotes Gallery; 146 Interior World/Fritz von der Schulenburg; 147 Lars Hallen/Design Press; 148 Quarto Publishing; 149 BAL/Partridge Fine Arts; 150 Ny Carlsberg Glyptotek, Copenhagen.
KEY: BAL = Bridgeman Art Library. RHPL= Robert Harding Picture Library
Background illustrations to chapter-opening pages:
pp 10-11: Samples of scagliola made by McCollin Bryan.
pp 54-5: Mosaic of the Flooding of the Nile from the Museo Archeologico, Palestrina, Italy.
pp 88-89: Fresco of the 'Staircase to Heaven or Hell' from the church at Sucevitsa, Romania.
pp134-135: Nineteenth-century red lacquer screen depicting oriental pastoral scene.